CALLED BY NAME

A MEMOIR

ANNA SHANE STADICK

For Abby

Thou hast turned for me my mourning into
dancing...
     Psalm 30:11

First, they took my things.

No purse, no shoes with laces. I took the string from my sweatpants and handed it over.

Then, in a side, padlocked room, they made me undress. The air-conditioner was on in November. I handed my clothes over, shivering, trying to cover myself as best I could.

"Over there." The nurse pointed to the corner of the room. "You need to squat."

"Squat?"

"We need to make sure you don't have anything up your vagina. Like a weapon or something."

"But I self-admitted."

"Protocol." She said something else; it was something funny that wasn't funny.

I squatted, looked at the raised bumps on my shaking legs, and wondered about the air-conditioner.

"Please put your arms by your sides."

I looked down at the droop of my stomach. Did she

think I was fat? I didn't want to be fat. It didn't matter if she saw the rest of me; I didn't want her to stare at my stomach. Not even I looked there.

I put my clothes on, and we went back into the hall where my fiancé waited. He was crying. He didn't want this for me. I didn't either—I told him that over and over and over—but I agreed to do what he said.

Somehow, out of some leftover sane corner of my mind, I knew what needed be done. I didn't understand it, but I could read his face: the terror. Was he afraid *for* me or *of* me?

"I don't want to leave you here." He couldn't stop crying.

"You have to get back to work."

"Can I call you?"

"You can call her." The nurse waited by the door. We didn't embarrass her; she saw this exchange all the time.

Rob left in what, to me, felt like slow motion. A few steps back, a wave, a few steps back.

Panic rose in my throat as the nurse led me through the small, darkened ward, pointing out the nurses' station, dining tables, and coloring table. I held my trembling hands against my chest. I hadn't expected to feel afraid—didn't realize I was mentally aware enough to feel any sort of trepidation. But I did—somehow, I understood the gravity of the situation despite the way my brain was buzzing. I could tell the nurse was trying to be kind; the way she murmured niceties and her presence were enough to keep me from ramming myself into a wall on the way to my room.

For the few remaining hours of the night, before

breakfast, I lay in the twin bed and wept quietly, trying not to wake the girl in the bed next to mine. Where was God? Where *was* He? Had He finally abandoned me, after all this time?

He was missing. Hiding behind the twisting, seething, inky black wires vibrating in my mind.

1

"I baptize you in the name of the Father."

I bent my knees, leaned back into his arms.

"In the name of the Son."

The pastor was farther behind me than I anticipated. For a second I thought I was falling backwards into empty air until the top of my head hit the middle of his chest. He led me back gently into the water, and I let my weight drop, my eight-year-old feet suspended.

Warm water covered my scrunched face, my torso, my hips. My hair became heavy, taking on the weight of the sacred. I continued to squeeze my eyes shut, counting the seconds. One, two.

Here am I, Lord. Use me, Isaiah, a prophet of the Old Testament, said.

Three, four. This was the moment of my belief, proof that this was *my* decision, in front of everyone. *Here am I, Lord. Use me.*

"And in the name of the Holy Spirit."

He pulled me up from the water, and I breathed in

deeply as my small feet stumbled for footing. I looked at the pastor, whose broad smile supported my choice of obedience to the Word of God, and then out into the crowd. I scanned the clapping congregation for my parents and spotted them a few rows in front of their usual spot. My mom waved, and my dad continued to take pictures.

This was it. I decided, for now and for the rest of my life: there was no undoing this.

The crowd continued to clap as I waded awkwardly towards the stairs. The long crimson robe clung to my legs as I reached for the thin towel hanging over the top of the railing.

Samuel, another prophet in the Old Testament, heard the voice of the Lord as a young child. He listened, uncertain of the voice. Was it his mother's? His mentor's? No, it was the Holy one, the one who already knew him by name.

"Speak, Lord," Samuel said, "For your servant is listening."

I swung the towel around my shoulders and went down the narrow back staircase that led into the restroom. I changed into my white dress, tights, and Mary Jane shoes and went to the mirror to braid my hair.

I was caught by the glow of my face in the mirror. I was eight years old, and I'd just made the biggest decision of my life. I felt giddy and nervous, quite certain of what I had done.

Anna, Anna.

I looked around, glanced for feet beneath the stalls. No one.

Anna, Anna.

The hairs on the back of my neck rose, and I braced myself against the sink, steadying myself as I felt weakness spread to my legs.

Anna, Anna.

I knew His voice. I was prepared for this moment. This was new, but I recognized the voice as if I'd heard it before. Suddenly, I was not eight years old. I was an infant, I was twenty. I was fifty. I was ageless, hovering in belief.

"Speak, Lord," I said aloud. My voice quivered against the silence of the room. "For your servant is listening."

No one answered.

But I knew He heard me, was with me now. I was His, and He was mine, and there was no escaping His hold, not even later, when I desperately wanted to.

≈

I was taught that God loved me. My parents' Christian faith was more than a list of rules to be followed on Sunday and forgotten by Friday. They taught me that having faith meant being in relationship, and I decided I wanted that relationship for myself.

In my understanding of the cosmic narrative, there is a deep divide between the divine and humanity. No one can be "good enough" to cross that divide; there is not a list of to-do's that earn us some ideal salvation. In some religions, prophets lead the way. In others, people must die a radical death to prove themselves. In the Christian narrative, God is the one who bridges the divide. Jesus

Christ, God incarnate, suffers, dies, and lives again, so that mankind can be reconciled to Him. Reconciliation, my family believed, looked like a personal, two-sided relationship.

There are many "extras" to the Christian faith, things that people make important when they shouldn't. There are things that are culturally misinterpreted, things that can cause more harm than good, and things that spur hatred instead of love.

Can a divinely inspired work carry human error? Is there space for metaphor, for different interpretations? Those are things I've wondered about; I still wonder.

But they're not that important—they're really not. Those are the extras.

There's one verse in the Bible that everyone in the Church knows, the one that I memorized in Sunday School classes. It's a verse that comes from the book of John, one of the gospel accounts that tells the story of the life of Jesus. It encapsulates Christianity; it gets rid of the extras; it is the core to the faith. *Because God loved the world, Jesus died for us.* Jesus suffered and died to bridge the divide, to give us salvation, and to believe in something that bizarre, that fantastical, that crazy, is to believe in something beautiful. Almost too remarkable.

But it is the suffering of Christ that I now find compelling. When Christ suffered, God was silent. There were no loud trumpets from heaven. There were no angels flying around the cross, giving him strength. Jesus cried out to God and heard nothing. *My God, my God, why have you forsaken me?* At the cross, God was silent.

But where was God more at work than at the cross?

God wasn't gone. It was the climax of His grand cosmic narrative. He was there, in the silence.

Even as a child, I liked the idea of a personal God. After my baptism—my external declaration of an internal faith—I prayed continuously. I wanted to be just like my great-grandmother, who sat for hours in her recliner talking to God. She told me she'd prayed for me every single day of my life. I wanted to know God like she did.

As a young child, I liked going to church. I liked the simplified Bible lessons; I liked the games we played and the books the teachers read aloud. I loved when we were given four Ritz crackers on a napkin with a Styrofoam cup of warm water during snack time, and, even more, I loved the Tootsie Rolls that were tossed my way when I correctly quoted a memorized verse. But above all this, I loved the way my Sunday School teachers talked about prayer, about how we could talk to Jesus whenever we wanted. They told us the story of Elijah and his search for God, in the book of 1 Kings. When Elijah stood upon a mountain, listening for God, a great strong wind passed by, breaking rocks into pieces. But God, Elijah realized, was not in the wind. After the wind, there was an earthquake. But God was not in the earthquake. Then there was a fire, and still no God. Then, finally, there was a gentle and barely audible blowing. There, in the almost silent stillness, was God, and He spoke. When I heard that story for the first time, I decided to start listening for God's still, small voice.

"Are you there, God? It's me, Anna."

I wanted, above all else, to hear Him.

I was a shy child, afraid to approach people and insecure about my everyday abilities, but I wasn't shy around God. I talked to Him in the mornings, throughout the day, and in the hour it took me to fall asleep each night.

"It's me, God. Let me tell you about my day."

"This is what I want, God. Do you understand?"

"I trust you, Jesus. Help me to trust."

I wanted to know Him. I wanted to love Him. I wanted to listen to Him speak into my life, and He did.

But I never really understood what God's love truly meant. I could parrot the Bible verses about love that I learned in Sunday School, as could any evangelical child of the 90's. *For God so loved the world...* The concept still seemed vague and untouchable, and maybe my faith, though sincere, was unable to hold something as heavy as God's love. I still felt like I needed to do something to earn it. This misunderstanding pervaded my faith, as if some other being wanted to put a barrier between me and my God. A demonic force? My own sin? I don't know.

By adolescence, I felt a desire, somewhere deep inside of me, that wanted more. God's love wasn't enough— somehow this thought crept into my psyche, unbidden. I don't know *where* it came from. I would continually seek God and consistently hear Him, yet I would not accept His love fully, no matter how unconditionally He offered it to me. Why? *Why* wasn't it enough?

I wanted love that I could actually see and hear clearly: a love I could physically hold and a love that could hold me back. I wanted it from my parents. I wanted it from my older sister and younger siblings. But, most of all, I wanted it from a boy.

Did I get this idea from movies? Books? I certainly read a lot of Christian romance novels, and they were formational in my understanding of love. In those kinds of books, the preachy prose barely veils that the love of a man is paramount to anything else.

As a romantic, I'd liked boys since I knew they existed, so it doesn't surprise me that someone caught my eye, and my heart, early on.

~

W e were going to rule the carrot kingdom, hand in hand. We'd marry and merge our family carrot businesses, farming the land into our happily ever after. Then we'd become missionaries, just like my parents had been early in their own marriage, and together we'd share the Gospel with unsuspecting foreigners, letting our light shine before others, just like the Bible taught. Daniel Markel didn't know it yet, but I had his entire life planned for him. Of course, I was the only one who thought this way at ten years old.

Our family carrot farms were the two reigning commercial carrot companies of the U.S., the two plants located just a few miles from each other in Bakersfield's fertile California farmland. After the baby carrot emerged in the early 90's, the businesses were friendly rivals.

Our family farm was officially started by my great-grandfather, although the history of the farm goes even further back than that. When I was a child, my grandfather served as CEO, and he prided himself on running his business by Christian principles. Employees were treated fairly. Bibles lay on the tables in the lobby of the office, free for the taking. Yearly dinners with guest Christian speakers were held for all the employees.

Every year, my private elementary school hosted a jog-a-thon, where children ran in circles to Christian pop music to raise money for the school. Every jog-a-thon, local companies donated food and drinks for the event. Sometimes Daniel's family farm would provide the snack-sized bags of carrots for each kid's brown paper lunch sack; other times, it was ours. The kids would eye Daniel and me suspiciously as they opened their sacks, seeing what carrot brand would prevail that year. Our farm? Quiet nods of approval in my direction.

My dad, in addition to being one of the owners, worked as the quality control manager at the carrot packing plant where he let me visit him when work wasn't too busy. As I rode around in his golf cart with a hair net and a long carrot in hand, I wondered if Daniel also visited his dad at his own plant. Did he watch the employees sort the little orange stubs on the conveyer belts? Or was he the type to linger by the secretary's candy bowl inside the air-conditioned office? Did his family keep Bibles in the lobby, like mine did? I didn't know Daniel at all.

I felt a sense of pride, a sense of unearned ownership as I trotted behind my dad in and out of the freezer room, eyes roving over the men lifting heavy boxes with machinery, as if they worked just for me. I don't know where I found this superiority—maybe it came from seeing our carrots in all of the grocery stores. We'd sell the company in a few years, and my superiority would leave me, but for now, it was there. I was sure Daniel felt the same.

∾

The secret attention I held for Daniel developed into a crush in the seventh grade. At the time, I was a thin fourteen-year-old, face inflamed with acne, desperate to fit in. No different from any other middle school girl.

My mom dealt with my pleas for popularity with surprising grace.

"I need a straightener for my hair. Daniel would want me to have straight hair."

"I need these pants. I prayed about it, and I think God wants me to have them. I think Daniel would want me to have them too." I thought this tactic would work on her.

"Mom, I shaved my legs. I didn't ask permission. But it was *absolutely* necessary, because I bet Daniel will notice."

Each time she responded with a cautionary tale of the dangers of trying to fit in. She remembered her own young crushes and wanted to spare me the waste of time —and the heartbreak. She reminded me that God cared about what was in my heart, not what I wore. I chose to find her stories irrelevant. This was the period of time in which my mom's and my relationship was barely more than tenuous. I responded to her in one of two extremes —passionate shows of love or extreme anger. She responded with equally passionate endearment or exasperation.

While my older sister Abby was closeted away in her room—she didn't want anything to do with our parents—I demanded my mom's attention in every way. We both had short tempers. I exploded because I wanted to; she exploded because she had to.

Years later, Abby told me she felt neglected at that time in our lives, like no one tried to get to know her. Mom was busy with our other siblings and didn't have time for us, Abby said. Emma was 8, Ian was 7, and Elly was 6—lots of kids means lots of things on the calendar. I guess five kids stretched Mom's time and attention. But I could only be incredulous at the difference in Abby's and my memories. Didn't have time for us? I commanded Mom's time. I dictated it and commandeered the intimacy.

Funny, how Abby and I remember our mother so differently. Memory is just like that, I guess. We remember what we want to remember.

It makes me wonder about the way I remember Daniel, the way I remember Lindsay, the way I remember the blue Gatorade.

~

I stood in the back of the line with my friend Hailey. We both stood on tiptoes, looking over shoulders to see what was left at the counter at the snack bar.

"Do you see any blue?" she asked me.

"One left, I think."

Blue Gatorade was something very special at Heritage Christian Junior High, the place where we raised our arms in chapel every Friday and prayed in math class. Of everything sold at the snack bar the mornings after electives, the blue Gatorade was the most valuable commodity. At some point in the school's arbitrary history, its refined flavor was declared the best. Yellow, of course, was good too. But not like blue.

"We'll never get it," Hailey whined.

"Don't lose hope," I told her, "There's always a chance."

But in a few minutes, it was gone, and instead of paying for a stale granola bar or an old packet of fruit snacks, Hailey and I left the line and went into our classroom early. We waited for our history teacher, a jolly man in glasses who wore pants that were too small for him.

"So, have you seen him yet?"

I nodded.

"And?"

"He was wearing a white shirt again."

"Well, hey, that's a good sign." She patted me on the shoulder.

"It is?"

"I think so. I mean, he could've worn red. Or green, or whatever."

"So?"

"I don't know. But it's a sign for something." Of course, the color of his shirt meant nothing, but Hailey and I were good at reading into things.

Hailey's face dropped into a grin, and she motioned to the door. It was Daniel.

Hailey wiggled her eyebrows up and down at me.

Then we saw Lindsay following him. Closely.

Usually, she sat with us. This time, however, she went to the desk beside his in the back. They were laughing about something, and I watched her touch him on the arm.

"Do you see what they're doing?" Hailey whispered. She poked me unnecessarily hard.

Flirting. I swallowed. They were flirting. "They're just talking, so what?"

"No, I mean, look what he's holding!"

Daniel took a swig from the bottle and held it out to Lindsay, who held it to her lips for a few seconds before taking a drink herself.

"Anna, they're sharing. *Sharing.*"

She was right. Daniel was sharing his blue Gatorade with Lindsay, which basically meant he was madly in love with her.

~

A year earlier, when I was thirteen, I was standing in front of my bedroom mirror, suitcase at my feet, staring. I wore a velvet brown tracksuit, a knock-off version of the Juicy Couture ones that the other girls wore on free dress days, the few days in the year when we were allowed to be out of uniform. A velvet tracksuit spelled lazy sophistication, the laid-back elegance I needed for the day's flight. I needed something that said I didn't try too hard but also something that said I was pretty enough to be noticed.

I toyed with my hair, making sure my messy bun was perfectly messy, but not too messy, adjusting the cheetah print ribbon that Lindsay had given me earlier that year.

"Perfect," I mouthed to the mirror.

Everything had to be perfect. Everything I'd packed had been chosen with care. Prayed over, even.

"God, please let me be pretty God, please let him like me. Please, please, please. I trust You no matter what. I trust that You have a plan. But please."

I was one of two students chosen to attend the leadership conference in Washington, D.C. Only the smartest, the best, really, were invited to a conference such as this. An honor, our principal told us. The other student was Daniel Markel.

I was getting five whole days with Daniel, alone. This trip would leave me with pure unadulterated time with the man of my dreams.

Hence, the painstakingly chosen outfits for the trip.

My mom dropped me off at the airport early, where Daniel, his mom, and his younger brother were waiting. Mrs. Markel volunteered to take us kids on the trip. While Daniel and I would be at the conference, his mom and brother would sightsee D.C.

Daniel's dad was there too. He looked like an older version of his son, though taller and grayer. He smiled and helped me with my overstuffed polka dot duffle bag, dragging it over to the security gate.

"You better keep these boys in line," he said.

"I will." I'd keep Daniel in line all right, whatever that meant.

His dad waved as we put our shoes back on at the end

of security. It's a moment that could've been insignificant, and it was, until later. I don't remember if Daniel waved back to his dad, if he said I love you. I want to remember that he did.

You got this, I thought. *He's right there. Just do it.*

Daniel sat near me on the plane, separated by just a mere aisle, the slightest separation to our romantic destiny. And all I needed to do was talk to him. To make him see that I was the one for him. I was a young teen in love; all I wanted was attention... from someone who didn't know I existed.

Think of something!

"Hey, Daniel?"

"Yeah?"

"Do you have the time?"

"It's 2:00."

"Oh. Okay. Thanks."

Do you have the time? Was that all I had? Not even, "What time is it?" like a normal person?

I didn't know the boy at all, really. I knew of the carrot business, of course, but that was about it. I'd just watched him from afar, inventing what I thought his personality might be like, based on the interactions he had with his friends. He was nice and quiet, I gathered, well respected in the grade. But anything else I knew I probably just imagined from what I wanted him to be. The attraction was contrived.

I pretended to read my Christian romance (Francine Rivers and I would be *best* friends if we ever met) for the next half hour or so, annoyed when the stewardess blocked my view, and watching out of the corner of my eye every time Daniel brought his Sprite to his lips. I needed to think of something better to say, something to start a conversation.

I would say, "Daniel, what's on your mind?"

And he would say, "You're *so* godly—I can see how much you love the Lord. And I've been thinking about how much I love you."

It could be so easy, so seamless. Instead it went, again, like this:

"Um, Daniel?"

"What?"

"Do you have the time?"

"2:40."

"Great. Thanks."

I asked him the same thing two more times, berating myself for my lack of creativity but still feeling a sense of my newfound boldness. At least I talked to him.

We got to the hotel later in the afternoon. It was a large hotel and the kind I guessed, from all the plush furnishings, that important people stayed in. There were mints at the front desk—the chocolate kind folded neatly in silver paper—and that meant the hotel was fancy.

The conference was to start the next morning. The two boys shared a hotel room that connected to the room I shared with Mrs. Markel. I'd only known her for a day, but I knew I loved her. She wore white tailored pants and a fitted blazer with gold trim, exactly the kind of clothes that I would wear when I grew up. Ever since the last baby, my mom usually wore sweatpants or gym shorts. I liked tailored pants.

We had an hour of downtime before dinner, which I

filled by straightening my hair, ironing my black velvet dress, and reapplying my lip gloss. I'd reel him in with looks, and then, once we talked, he'd see that there was more to me.

I sat next to him at dinner and then again on the floor of his room as we watched a movie. Still, I could find no words, nothing but the benign, "This food is good," and, "I have to use the restroom." Pathetic. But I had the rest of the week. And maybe Daniel was just nervous. Maybe he secretly liked me and was just scared to talk to me too. That could be, right? Maybe we'd both find the words. Maybe we'd end up talking for hours. Maybe. God would help me.

I went to bed hopeful, knowing that the start of the conference was going to bring me time alone with Daniel. Knowing what I was feeling just had to be love.

Hours later, I woke up to sobbing. It was startling, and I just lay there for a few minutes, my limbs heavy. I reached for my phone. 3:00 in the morning. Rolled over. Blinked, adjusting to the darkness. The air in the room felt heavy.

Mrs. Markel was crouched on the floor, knees to chest, holding her cell phone to her ear. She rocked back and forth, crying.

I tried to make out what she was saying on the phone, but her crying made it hard to understand. I wouldn't even call it crying—she was *wailing*. I'd never seen an adult cry like that. Not even my parents.

I sat up and stared. What was I supposed to do? When she hung up the phone, she flung herself forward onto the floor.

"Brian. Brian." She called her husband's name again and again.

This was an adult, a mom. This was grief, and I'd never seen it before. What was I supposed to do?

I immediately began to pray. I didn't know what to pray, not exactly, so I said the Lord's Prayer over and over. *Deliver us from evil. Deliver us from evil. Deliver us from evil.*

Minutes passed, then an hour. When her sobs turned into hiccupping, I got out of bed to get a water bottle. I'd offer her some water. That would help, right? But I couldn't get the lid off. My hands were slick with sweat—I hadn't noticed that my whole body was covered in cold wetness. Chills raced up and down the back of my neck. I set the bottle back down quietly. She still hadn't noticed me.

I looked at my phone. 4:00.

At 4:30, her cries subsided, and she got on the phone again, this time to book a flight home. I listened to her plead with the airline and watched as she shuffled around the room, throwing things haphazardly into her suitcase. She put her white pants back on, and they looked wrinkled and gray in the dim light.

Then, she looked at me. It wasn't embarrassment in her eyes or anger. Rather, it was a startled discomfort. Without saying a word, she told me I wasn't supposed to be there. I was the undeserving witness to something too private.

"You need to pack up. Our flight is in an hour and a half," she said.

I nodded. My throat felt dry. I couldn't say anything.

"I have to go into that room," she pointed to the

connecting door, "and tell my sons that their father is dead."

I nodded without looking at her, embarrassed that I'd seen her cry.

I texted my parents to let them know I'd be coming home early. My mom probably had her cell on her nightstand, because she answered quickly, assuring me over and over that everything would be okay. My dad texted me from his phone to tell me he was praying for us.

Only ten minutes passed before Mrs. Markel reemerged from her sons' room. Daniel and his brother followed her, wheeling their small bags behind them. I didn't want to look at Daniel's pale, blank face, but I did. I couldn't bear to look at him, and I couldn't bear not to.

On the plane, I didn't ask him for the time. I wonder if he felt me looking at him, but he probably didn't. He stared at the movie playing in the headrest in front of him, a stupid cartoon, and his eyes stayed wide and frozen in shock.

I felt absolutely helpless. I wanted to say something. I wanted to tell him I was so sorry, that I was praying for him, that I cared. Instead, I maintained the silence we were accustomed to.

At the time, I hoped he sensed my support; I felt we were connected in that instant. There we were, both silent, sitting side by side. Looking back now, I really don't think I was supposed to be there in that intimate moment of his life. Somehow, I got misplaced in time, stuck where I didn't belong.

A few days later, I found my dad in his garden. He was bent over some beets with a spade and a bucket, humming one of the hymns we sang in church. He sang hymns all the time. Around the house. Even when he went running. It frustrated my mom, when she was completely out of breath, that he could sing and run at the same time.

I hadn't talked much about what'd happened, didn't know how. I felt bad that I hadn't been able to attend the conference after all, hadn't been able to brag about what I learned. I felt worse that I hadn't been able to talk about what happened that night. When I'd arrived home that morning, I went straight to my room and cried—finally what had happened was starting to sink in. My mom knocked gingerly at my door, came in, and held me until I quieted. But I hadn't been able to talk about it. Now, I wanted to.

Mr. Markel suffered a heart attack, had died on the spot. The last time Daniel had seen his dad had been at the airport. It wasn't even a proper goodbye.

"Why did God let that happen?" I asked my dad even before he turned around,. "Why do bad things happen?"

He sighed. "I don't know, Anna."

"Do you think there's a reason for everything?" I'd heard that before in Sunday School.

"I'd like to think that. But I'm not sure."

I'd expected him to say yes. "You're not sure?"

"I don't know."

I needed a reason. I needed some sort of sense, some order out of what happened that night in D.C. I'd wanted that week to be a time to fall in love, and, instead, someone died.

"Dad, I think I know the reason."

"What's that?"

"Maybe his dad died so that Daniel and I would fall in love. Maybe the death will bring us together. We're bonded now."

My dad winced. "Honey..."

"Maybe not. I don't know. But maybe."

Daniel and I *were* bonded, I thought. We didn't need to speak to one another. The two of us just *knew*. I was sure of it.

"But, Dad, I still don't get it. Why doesn't God tell me why this happened? I've been praying, but I can't hear an answer."

"God still works in things we don't understand, even when He's quiet," he said.

"Like when you're sick?"

"Um." He looked away.

"Mom says you're sick again."

"It comes and goes lately."

Dad sometimes couldn't come out of the bedroom because he was feeling a "terrible sadness." Mom called it a sickness, but he didn't look sick to me. That was the reason we'd left our home in China to come back to California when I was just a toddler. I didn't know what happened, but it had to do with his sickness. His terrible sadness, whatever it was. I was curious, of course, but smart enough to know that it wasn't my business. I just didn't want what happened to Daniel's dad to happen to mine.

"Hey, Anna? Listen to me. God helps us when we're having a hard time. He helps me. He's going to help Daniel and his family. And He'll help you too."

"Nothing is wrong with me."

"I know. I mean someday."

I left the conversation a little confused. *I* never wanted to be sad or sick. I mean, I was sick sometimes, but not in the way Dad was talking about.

Daniel's dad's death didn't threaten my belief in God. It'd only wavered for a moment. That night, I prayed that God would comfort Daniel, that my Dad could be happy again, and that nothing bad would ever happen to me.

For the rest of the year and into the next, I kept my eye on Daniel. We would never talk to each other again, but I saw an invisible string from my heart to his, even as a year passed, and felt the gentle tugging whenever I went unnoticed.

~

But if this a story with Daniel in it, it also has Lindsay, who came over after school on the day of the blue Gatorade incident.

Lindsay was a goddess, one of my best friends, and she would haunt me for the rest of my life. In the fourth grade, she had short, silky, brown hair that I was allowed to stroke three times a day—no more than three. When I cut mine to match hers the summer before the fifth grade, I arrived to find, horrified, that she'd grown hers out past her shoulders.

She was a popular girl, the beloved and beautiful one

in my grade. She was the first to wear a bra, first to get her period, and first to have a boyfriend. Lindsay wasn't the type to go to church every Sunday, so she introduced me to "sinful" things, like spaghetti-strap tank tops, bikinis, and shorts with words on the butt. Things I wasn't allowed to wear.

I didn't want to be like Lindsay. I wanted to *be* Lindsay; I wanted the boys to like me like they did her. I wanted to be beautiful.

~

Lindsay was the first person to introduce me to makeup, to what beauty really was, a couple years earlier, right around the time my crush developed.

She'd patted her bathroom counter years before and had told me to hop up. I let my feet dangle off the counter and then flinched, surprised, when she came at me with an eyelash curler.

"I'm going to make you beautiful," she said as she caked heavy foundation and powder and concealer and eye shadow and mascara and eyeliner and blush *and* bronzer onto my fourteen-year-old face.

"If only the boys could see you now!" She pointed to my face in the mirror. "*Now* they'll like you."

~

The big Constitution test was in just a few days, and I'd promised to help her study at my place. I loved an excuse for Lindsay to come over to my house, even if Daniel *had* shared his Gatorade with her.

Lindsay and I went through our Constitution flashcards ten times. I knew I was ready and she wasn't, but we quit when she complained that her head hurt from all the studying. We were sitting on my bed in my room, papers and folders scattered at our feet, and I was telling her about how it was important to read the Bible every day, like I was often told in Sunday School. I often shared verses with her, verses I'd memorized and committed to following.

"Hey, Anna, I have something I need to tell you," she interrupted.

"Okay."

"It's very serious. But I know you'll understand." Her words were cautionary, but she was smiling, anticipating the sound of her secret out loud.

"Okay..."

"I think I like Daniel."

She liked Daniel? My Daniel? I thought of the blue Gatorade. I should've known. I *did* know.

"Don't be mad. I know you've liked him for a long time, but—but I can't help it. I thought I should tell you."

Once again, I was at a loss for words. Why couldn't I stand up for myself? I should've been angry, but, in that instant, all I felt was defeat. It didn't matter what I felt. Lindsay had already won—*she* was the beautiful one— and I knew it.

I don't remember what we said after that. I think I changed the topic. When I caught her looking at me intently, I asked her what was wrong, half hoping she would say she was kidding and half hoping she wouldn't bring up his name again.

"Oh, it's just that I think you're doing your makeup wrong again. You're not doing it how I told you."

"What?"

"You're not covering your acne very well. It's very obvious. Let me help you." She led me into the bathroom, wet a washcloth, and rubbed my forehead. When some of the pimples started bleeding, she told me how to wash my face properly, and patted my face dry with another washcloth.

After she left, I didn't know if I was crying over Daniel or over my humiliation. I went back to the mirror.

"God...?"

You are fearfully and wonderfully made.

No, I'm not, God. No, I'm not.

∿

Over the course of the next few weeks, I watched Lindsay and Daniel closely, but from afar. There were more blue Gatorade exchanges and some talking between classes, sitting next to each other in chapel and passing notes in science. I watched them play basketball from a bench against the wall, envying her each time she made a basket. If only I were good at sports. Why couldn't I be more athletic?

I knew I didn't have a chance. Not against Lindsay, not how he looked at her. Big boobs, perfectly applied lip gloss. Even her cuticles were manicured expertly. I knew, because she had done her nails in my own bathroom.

I tried doing my hair differently and changing the color of my eye shadow from blue to purple. I even tried lingering by his locker after school. I couldn't bring myself to say a word. Deep down I knew I was more than looks, though my insecurities were only steadily increasing as I continued to compare myself with Lindsay, and I couldn't bear the thought of him rejecting the rest of me too. I couldn't go on pretending that Daniel and I were secretly connected.

Lindsay's lessons on beauty became inescapably intertwined with the way I would think about romance. *If only the boys could see you now.* I'd hear her words and feel that same face-scrubbing shame whenever I felt unnoticed. If a boy didn't notice me, there was probably something wrong with me. I needed to change.

~

Every morning before school, I'd sit by my window in my faux fur pink chair and pray for God to intervene on my behalf. I knew that even though God had wars and famines to take care of, He also promised to take care of me. Some days I'd pray that He would make Daniel notice me over Lindsay. Other days I'd pray that God would take away any affection I felt. Then I'd remember my dad's mysterious sadness, and I'd pray for that too.

Fourteen was probably my most pious year; I rededicated my life to God at a church youth event and joined the kid's choir where we sang worship songs in our best Sunday clothes. I was still heavily rooted in much of the legalism—excessive adherence to rules. If I were good enough, God would reward me. That's what I thought. That's not what my parents believed, but I picked the idea up somewhere, I'm just not sure where. I was more dutiful in my prayer and devotions than I'd ever be again, more sure of God's presence than I could even claim now. My parents reminded me again and again that there was no checklist that I needed to perfect in order to earn God's approval, but I was naturally driven to do everything the "right way." I was type A and a perfectionist.

At first, I wanted Mr. Markel's death to mean something more than just the tragic cycle of life. I wanted it to be about *me*. My pain. My world was small, and it revolved around myself—somehow, Daniel and the death of his father had to fit into that small world.

But when Lindsay told me she and Daniel were officially dating the afternoon after the Constitution test, I realized none of that fit into my world as perfectly as I wanted it to.

Those people at church—the ones who said everything happened for a reason? They were wrong. Insisting upon having a reason is only a flimsy way of trying to understand the unknowable, the pointlessness. Mr. Markel's death was senseless.

Sometimes death just happens. Pain happens.

But even at fourteen, when I didn't fully understand that concept, I still knew God could work through senselessness—He *had* to. What else could I cling to?

Seven years later, lying on my bed in a dorm room, I chatted on the phone with Lindsay. We hadn't talked since junior high, and it felt strange to hear her voice, the same but not. I'd been doing a writing project for one of my classes, a writing assignment on childhood friendships. As a part of the assignment, I was required to talk to someone from my past with whom I'd lost contact.

Lindsay was the first person to come to mind when the project was presented in class. Her words about beauty stuck, shaped the way I thought about myself— the writing would come easily enough, I thought. I remembered her as the angel on my shoulder whispering insecurities into my ear. I didn't want closure—I wanted to write a story that gave me a sense of vengeance. I remembered her as evil, myself as the victim of abuse. But when I finally talked to her on the phone, I was faced with someone entirely different: someone kind.

"Do you know something?" Lindsay asked me halfway into the conversation.

"What?" I picked at a piece of fuzz on my pillow, pinning the phone between my shoulder and ear.

"I still have a note you gave me. You told me that you'd pray for me every single day of my life. You told me to *always* follow God."

"I don't remember that. That's hilarious."

I actually did remember the note. I was embarrassed at both how silly and overly devout it was. Anna Shane, Mrs. Martin Luther. I was also embarrassed that I'd forgotten to follow through on my young, heartfelt promise.

Lindsay then went on to talk about what a large impact I'd had on her life, how she'd always remember my kindness and our friendship.

"You were always talking about God. He was so *real* to you," she said. "You helped me so much. Do you remember that?"

I didn't know what to say. How is it that our memories of one another could be so different? I remember the pain I felt she caused me, while she remembered me with fondness? Was the hurt she caused me really that unintentional? I felt betrayed by my memory. *We remember what we want to remember.*

We wrapped up the conversation, but not before I heard about her current boyfriend.

Daniel Markel, the carrot man.

They went to the same high school and then the same college, where, years later, they were together again.

"I'm so happy for you," I said, actually meaning it. It surprised me, because I hadn't felt happy in a long time.

Once we hung up, I went to my mirror and leaned in close to study the acne scars on my face. Still there. Still taunting me.

"God...? You there?" I started to pray, still staring at the mirror like I'd done all those years ago after my baptism.

I created your inmost being. You are fearfully and wonderfully made.

God was still here, with me.

After a few minutes, I went to my bookshelf and stood on tiptoe to reach the Bible I hadn't read in weeks. Maybe reading a Psalm would help my terrible sadness go away.

2

I felt heavy and numb. I was like a wilting flower, lifeless and lost of my color. I tried praying, but depression made it hard to hear God like I once had.

I spent time crouched in the mechanical closet in my basement that July, the summer before my freshman year of high school, knees to chest against the wall. It was cool and dark and silent, no light or sound penetrating the metal doors. That summer was even hotter than usual, but the hiding had less to do with the heat than with the depression. I stayed in the closet for an hour at a time, crying about nothing or allowing my mind to go blank.

I spent a lot of time in that cool darkness as the days brought me closer and closer to school. I was supposed to be in the basement, scanning old pictures into my mom's computer. Quite the boring job for the summer, but, because of my time in the closet, the job took two months instead of a few weeks.

Still, I prayed. I clung to the verses in my Bible that

spoke of hope, encouraged to know I wasn't alone. I memorized them and whispered them softly to myself over and over in that closet. Depression was lonely, but at least I had God on my side. It was enough to keep me from pulling my hair out—an urge that floated through my thoughts constantly, like the voice that told me to hurt myself in other ways.

I knew that my dad often suffered from depression like me—he was depressed now, in fact. When I was younger, they called it a "sadness" or a "sickness," but as I got older, they simply called it what it was: Depression, a demon with a will of its own.

His depression paralyzed him, preventing him from making any sort of decision. He stopped working at the carrot plant abruptly and, instead of finding new work, floundered into a permanent state of uncertainty. He lost all momentum and couldn't handle thinking about the future, which left our family in a state of limbo. Mom told us to be patient with him. Dad just "needed to make up his mind," she said. I could see that she was frustrated, that it affected her, even though she tried to hide it. Still, she never showed anything but love and patience for him, which I admired. In retrospect, I think her frustration just came out of worry.

Dad hid it remarkably well, from me and especially from my younger siblings. We loved that he was home more, not tied up with things at work. Sometimes he secluded himself in his bedroom, but for the most part, he put on a very brave face and managed to laugh at the jokes at the dinner table. He was involved in our lives and never let his feelings get in the way of being a good father.

I often found him out in the backyard, puttering around his garden in a big floppy hat, singing those familiar hymns while he worked; he said they helped him with his bad thoughts. *Come thou fount of every blessing, tune my heart to sing thy praise... Teach me some melodious sonnet, sung by flaming tongues above...*

I didn't know that there'd been another side, something even more sinister, to his mental illness. My depression seemed like an isolated event because it was the first time it had happened. I couldn't fathom that it might one day define my life.

I tried praying about it, but I felt like I was talking to a wall. Why was it so hard? I *knew* God was with me, but I couldn't *hear* Him.

I found relief on my bike, which was funny for the girl who hated anything remotely physical. (I especially hated anything that required you to hit, throw, or catch a ball.) We lived on a golf course, in one pocket neighborhood of a larger gated community. I'd finally figured out that riding my parents' golf cart around wasn't as cool as it was at ten years old, so the bike—much cooler—got me out of the house as the cart once had. I wasn't very good at biking. I maybe went ten miles an hour, at most, but I liked it. On my bike, I didn't really think about anything. Biking just allowed me to *feel*. I could feel the wind on my way down a hill or the tension in my legs on the way up, and it was enough to replace the numbness.

❧

I'd wanted to start the first day of high school happy, the senseless and oppressive heaviness just a thing of summer. I pictured myself walking onto the school campus smiling at the handsome boys—my future boyfriends—and listening to other girls' comments about how amazing my clothes were. It was the first year my mom gave a larger allowance, a privilege granted after my graduation from junior high, and I had every intention of spending all of it on clothes. The only problem was that the depression hadn't left. I didn't feel like buying anything. The cash sat on my dresser as I wore the same T-shirt and gym shorts each day.

The day I registered for classes was the day I learned that students had to play at least one sport a year unless we opted for a P.E. class. This meant death either way, so I picked a tennis racquet I could hide behind.

For the first few weeks of practice before school started, the energy I needed to make friends with the other girls on the team didn't surface as I'd hoped. I couldn't even force myself to smile at the end of a practice, when I could finally go home. The other girls were annoyed that I used my racquet as a shield instead of actually going for a backhand. To put it another way, I wasn't the ideal doubles partner.

I was so embarrassed, that I arrived late and left early just so that I wouldn't have to talk to anyone, complaining of conveniently timed stomachaches. I faked whatever I had to in order to get out of socializing. Fortunately for me, a broken arm got me off the courts.

I was taking my anger out on my bike, pedaling furiously uphill near hole seven. My front wheel hit gravel, my bike jerked to the left, and I fell hard. I picked myself up and biked even harder, angry at the tingling pain in my limbs. Tears clouded my vision, and I lost control of my bike again, this time landing on my right arm.

I could call the broken arm a bike accident, but I could also call it divine intervention for the team that wanted to win without me. I still had to go to those stupid matches, but the girls did seem to like me more when I handed out Powerade, my new required contribution.

Showing up on the first day of school with a giant white cast on my arm doesn't sound so bad. But having to ask a scary upperclassman I didn't know to help me open the lock on my locker three times and getting stuck in the bathroom because I couldn't zip my skirt with my left hand—yeah, the cast made the first day pretty miserable for the girl wanting to make, not a good, but rather a fabulous impression. In lieu of any impression, I started high school broken in more ways than one.

~

My sister Abby and I always arrived at school with a few minutes before the bell, and I'd get to French just in time, enough to analyze the teacher's outfit —my ritual for the beginning of class. White button-down shirt stretched at the bust, revealing a large tan bra, just a tad too see-through. If it weren't for her frizzy blonde hair and god-awful orange lipstick, the look might've been alluring, even to me.

I didn't talk to anyone in class. In French and history,

not a word, just like in science and math. I just came and went silently, turned in my work early, and got the A's I wanted. I wasn't just a moody teenager—something was off. I wasn't myself. I still felt numb and sad and had that faint voice in the back of my head telling me I'd be better off dead.

In our school's chapel service? I sat in the back and watched kids fiddling with their cell phones, no interest whatsoever in whatever speaker was there that day. I didn't have much interest in it either. I couldn't explain why, but God was feeling farther away than usual, so if He wasn't making an effort, why should I?

After chapel, I had my one class with my junior high friend, Hailey. I was happy that she sat with me, and I listened as she gushed about the drama within her new friend group—the boyfriends and breakups, the inside jokes. My job was to nod and smile, hint that maybe I could sit with them sometime, and then tell her no, I didn't like any guy yet. I didn't have enough energy to make new friends, and she slowly stopped trying to include me.

In Old Testament class, we were greeted by Mr. Gary's handshakes at the door, the teacher who somehow got away with Abercrombie jeans and a gold chain necklace. His class was easy for me, a perk of being a Sunday School kid, and it won me favor with some of the sophomore girls who needed to copy my answers.

I remember them because they were my saviors, inviting me to sit with them after class at lunch a month into the school year. They didn't talk to me much the rest of the day, but it was nice to have a place to sit at the tables outside the gym.

Abby usually sat in her car to eat while listening to an audiobook and had actually invited me a few times to join, surprising both of us. My sister and I weren't exactly getting along lately. Which means we weren't getting along at all. A few arguments into the car lunches, and she didn't care if I sat alone outside. So the sophomore girls saved me in their lunchtime invitation.

But there wasn't much eating involved at lunchtime.

My lunch started with a turkey and cheese sandwich, a bag of tortilla chips, carrots, and an apple.

But then, a few weeks later, as I emptied my brown paper bag onto the table, I noticed that the other girls weren't eating anything.

"Not hungry."

"On a diet."

"Not a big lunch girl."

So, the next time I emptied my brown paper bag, it was a sandwich, carrots, and an apple—no chips.

Later, I learned that the girls in my class—the freshman girls, that is—were practicing "Starvation Tuesday." Class bonding or something. It made me feel uncertain of my eating habits. How much did I have to change?

❧

It was November, it was foggy, and Abby and I were fighting about the predestination of dead babies on our way to school. (I have no idea who thought what.) Sisters, I've heard, fight about a lot of things, and Abby and I brought our differing theologies into our forty-five-minute car rides to school. Predestination, interpretation of Scripture, whatever. She was older, so she assumed she was right. *I* assumed that I was smarter, which meant I was the one in the right. Really, we had no idea what we were talking about.

While I will probably forget a lot about that lonely year in my life, I don't think I will ever forget those car rides, where my anger and desperation were directed solely at my older sister.

If we weren't yelling at one another, she sat in sullen silence as I made useless chatter that I knew would annoy her. Abby was a senior and most knew her to be the outgoing, effusive girl with lots of friends. I knew Abby as the she-devil that she was, cold and uncaring behind closed doors. I told her so, which is probably why she didn't like me very much. In seriousness, I just wanted Abby to like me as much as she did her friends at school and church. Sucked into her new volleyball clique, I was seeing Hailey less and less, and as depression continued to fill my thoughts, I needed a new confidante, someone to make me feel less alone as we drove each day to the place I didn't like very much.

I tried in my own way, I guess, but Abby didn't try back. "You're so mean," meant, "I want to be friends with you." "I'm smarter than you," meant, "I want you to admire me." Somehow, I thought, poking and exposing Abby's flaws would win me her respect. If she saw me as intelligent, she would love me.

After fuming about my fight with Abby the entire day, I found Hailey after school, hoping to commiserate about how terrible high school was turning out to be. I wanted to tell her about Abby too—we used to always talk about how mean she was—but hadn't had a chance yet.

"How was your day? Isn't this all so great?" She was stuffing things into her backpack in a hurry. Books, mechanical pencils, an oversized water bottle.

"Um, I don't know. With the cast and everything..."

"Oh. *Totally* sucks."

"Yeah."

"Did you know Zach asked me out yesterday? He's been coming to our games."

"Really? I didn't know." I waited for her to say more.

"So, do you maybe want to come over later?" I ventured, when she didn't. In junior high, if we weren't at each other's homes in the afternoon, we'd be on the phone every night at eight. We'd gossip a bit, and then I'd give her the answers to our math homework problems.

"Sorry. I have practice. And then Taylor and Stefani are coming over to swim."

I waited for her to invite me.

"So, I'll see you tomorrow?" She swung her bag over her shoulder and picked up the volleyball that sat by her feet.

"Okay, yeah." I didn't know what I was feeling, but it was sinking deeper and deeper into my chest. I left for the courts, picking up a few packs of Powerade and filling up the cooler with ice on my way. It wasn't exactly easy, you know, with the arm and all. I'd *finally* be getting the cast off next week, but it couldn't come soon enough.

It turned out that that was the day for team pictures. All the girls were wearing their new uniforms, short white skirts and blue tanks with glittery letters, ponytails high with blue and silver ribbons. I asked my coach, holding the now empty box, for my uniform, and she looked at me, embarrassed, and said they'd forgotten to order one for me. They still let me stand in the picture. In the back. Honestly, I was just glad the season was ending.

~

At lunch: No chips. Half a sandwich without the cheese, carrots, sometimes an apple.

One of the sophomore girls announced she'd finally reached her weight goal. "Maybe just five more pounds," she said. "My boyfriend doesn't want me to be fat."

The next day, I didn't need a brown paper bag. Just carrots. I carefully ate each one in half and threw the rest away. The other girls didn't say anything, but I imagined that they approved.

As the amount of food I ate started to plummet, so did the numbers on my bathroom scale. As I grew thinner in my clothes, I grew fatter in the mirror. I finally understood: boyfriends hated fat girls.

Even the girls at church, the ones with clear skin, the ones at Bible Study on Wednesday nights? They were on diets. And they all had boyfriends.

I was too fat. Ninety pounds—barely anything—and too fat.

I ate normally at dinner—parental interference would only make things worse. When I thought my mom was catching on, I made a point of pouring large bowls of cereal in the mornings. When she left the kitchen, I dumped them into the disposal, leaving just a few cheerios in the bowl to make it look like I'd missed a few when I rinsed out the milk.

~

I stood naked in front of the mirror, fingernails digging into the skin on my stomach. I didn't see the nice legs or shapely curves. Just the middle, just the bulge.

You are fat. Disgusting. Scum.

My eyes eventually moved to my face. My gaze didn't take in the pretty green eyes or the freckles on my nose. Only the inflamed red dots that studded my forehead and chin.

Hideous. Loser. No one likes you. You *don't like you.* The voice was not my own. It was not God's.

I reveled in the self-pity, recognizing and hating it and wanting to feel like a victim all at the same time. I avoided the mirror and worshiped it, looking at my stomach and worsening acne but never into my eyes.

God wasn't absent at the time, merely in the background—for a while, anyway. Depression is quiet, but it is louder, sometimes, than faith.

~

I n kindergarten, the boy I dubbed "Kissy-Boy" liked to chase me around the playground, warning me that if I were caught, I'd be kissed, a dreadful consequence no respectable five year old would desire. I loved it, though, and even though his little obsession only lasted a week, I remember the pursuit well. Once, he did catch me. I squealed, but he just stared at me in embarrassment, the follow-through unbearable for the both of us. He didn't chase me after that.

It just so happened that Kissy-Boy (his name was Aaron) sat in front of me in Study Hall. I don't think he remembered me at all, which saved us both some awkwardness. I listened to him talk as I worked, his opinions way over the top about anything.

"Bush is the most idiotic president we've ever had."

"Whoever doesn't like Bush is stupid. He's done more for this country than you could ever dream of doing."

"Has anyone ever *seen* global warming? How do we know it's not just one big joke?"

"Anyone who didn't get an A on that biology quiz obviously didn't try."

Aaron was certain that Neil Armstrong was a paid actor and made sure the entire room heard his thoughts about the Hollywood moon. The guy knew everything about everything and if you contradicted him... Well. You were clearly the idiot.

Quite honestly, I don't know why the small crush developed. He was annoying and overbearing. It was a crush born out of necessity rather than real admiration. I didn't like him, not truly, just couldn't make myself. But if I could fool myself into thinking he liked me, then I could also fool myself into feeling wanted, feeling beautiful. This pretend-crush made Study Hall the one class I wanted to go to and his opinions more important than they ought to have been.

I listened to Aaron and his friend Josiah talking one

day in Study Hall. This conversation I do remember, their words burned permanently into my mind.

They were talking about girls they thought were *hot*. I didn't think they'd look my way or anything, but I was curious to know Aaron's type.

I already knew most boys didn't like fat girls. And I was working on that. But maybe I'd fit other criteria.

"What about Stefani?" Josiah brought up another girl to Aaron.

"Definitely hot. Smoking."

"Angela? She's pretty cute, right?" Josiah asked.

"Are you serious? Eww. Hello? ACNE." Aaron made a face.

"Oh, yeah, you're right. Gross." Josiah laughed and listed another girl.

My face fell, and I touched my forehead, where the inflamed bumps protruded the skin. I had acne. I was gross.

I didn't even like him! Why did I care? But I was gross.

And with everything else going on in my life, I needed him to like me.

I raised my hand, asked to be excused, and went into the bathroom. I wadded up brown paper towels and doused them with water, packing them down into a rough wet ball. No one else was in the bathroom, so I stood before the mirror, staring at my face for a few seconds.

An overwhelming sense of self-loathing felt heavy, like a bowling ball sitting tight in my chest. It was all-consuming, washing over me and clinging to every inch of my skin.

Do it. Hurt yourself. You're hideous. That voice, always callous, always biting.

I started scrubbing as hard as I could, harder and harder.

No one will ever love you.

My face began to bleed, and I kept scrubbing. No, this was not God's voice. But I listened anyway.

Leave your life.

Tiny trickles of blood met my eyebrows, and I looked at them, the proof of the pain I could not put into words. My penance for feeling this way.

I stopped scrubbing, rinsed my face in the sink. It stung. I arranged my bangs to fall over my forehead, pulled up the hood on my sweatshirt, and walked out with my head down.

That night I found myself back in the mechanical closet, but this time the depression was exponentially worse.

"God, why did you make me so ugly?" I whispered into my hands. "I need you right now." He was supposed to care about the little things, wasn't He?

"God, listen. I need you to take these feelings away."

"God, help me."

"Where are You? Why are You silent?"

~

My family took a trip to Hawaii over a school holiday break. Palm trees and white sand welcomed us, but I wasn't too pleased about sharing a room with my four siblings.

One night, the hotel spa was hosting a "teen night," a dimly lit room with spas filled with rock salts of all different colors. I begged Abby to come with me.

"It'll be fun. I don't want to go by myself. I *can't* go by myself. I'll die if I go by myself," I said. "Please?"

"I don't want to. Go by yourself." She had a headache, but I didn't care. I wouldn't understand the extent of her migraines, the chronic pain, until years later. I didn't want to be alone. I told her she was terrible and threatened that I would still go and hate her for it.

I did go alone, and I sat by myself in the back of a hot tub, watching other older kids flirt and laugh. I felt self-conscious in my swimsuit and waited until everyone had left before I got out of the tub. I came back to the room with mascara smeared across my face, smelling like a combination of sulfur and chlorine. I wanted to yell at my sister—*like me, like me, like me!* Towards the end of the week, my mom caught me trying to throw up my dinner in the bathroom after a luau. The imaginary bulge in my black and white flowered dress was too much for me as I passed a hotel hallway mirror: I went straight to the bathroom with a finger down my throat. My throat burned and my eyes watered, but I kept trying, over and over, until I gagged up only spit. (I would never be a good bulimic—I'd have to resign myself to simply not eating anything.) I hadn't locked the door, as if I actually wanted my mom to find me, to stop me. Maybe it was an over-the-top need for attention, or maybe I was just begging for help. I don't know. Maybe those are the same things?

When we returned home, my mom sat with me in my room and preached quietly about self-love. When I didn't seem to listen, my parents put me into counseling. They said they were worried about me, that my actions could be a warning sign for something more dangerous. What was more dangerous? They said I could be concerned about *that* when I was older, if I needed to.

I acted like I was embarrassed, but I was pleased with the special treatment. I went to see Susan on Tuesdays, sitting in one of her large green armchairs with a cup of warm chai tea in hand. The room was warm, and it was difficult to keep my eyes open.

I learned from my parents that I'd actually been to see Susan as a ten year old, something I don't remember. I vaguely remember coloring in her office, but I think I only remember that because they told me I did. Apparently, I'd been showing signs of an eating disorder—an eating disorder, when I was *ten*. Why? I didn't understand. I felt bad for my younger self, and sad that, years later, I was in the exact same place. But Susan and I ended up talking about the depression, not the eating issue.

Abby and I didn't really talk about the counseling appointments, not as much as I wanted to. I wanted her to understand why I was so sad and why that should make her love me again. I assumed she would think me annoying, the usual drama queen. (Which is valid, because I usually was.)

Abby was an enthusiastic extrovert at church and at school but sank into depression whenever she was home. She complained of headaches every week, but never advocated for herself in order to get professional help. I didn't understand her pain at the time: Drama Queens don't see much farther than themselves.

In counseling, we addressed the sadness that was finally beginning to dissipate. Nothing warranted medication, especially since my depression was lightening, but Susan prescribed breathing practices (1-2-3-deep breath in, 1-2-3-deep breath out) that I promised I'd try but didn't. My problem was somewhere in my thoughts, I figured, not in my breathing. I never tried anything she suggested, but talking through things with her each week *did* help me. After each session, I left feeling a little less heavy. Maybe counseling was an answer to my prayers. Maybe God was listening after all.

~

My Aunt Kathy, my mom's youngest sister, came to visit in the spring. She arrived with only a small suitcase. Her eyes were sunken into her face; her cheekbones were more than prominent. She'd lost at least thirty pounds since the last time I'd seen her. Her once full figure looked emaciated. "The divorce diet," she called it.

A year before, my aunt learned that her husband had been cheating on her. Throughout her entire marriage. With women she'd called friends. The divorce was messy.

For the week she was there, she kept to herself. Sometimes she came to meals, sometimes she didn't. She went about the house like a quiet shadow. Mom told me she was severely depressed.

My aunt went on long walks around the neighborhood. Sometimes she was gone for as long as three hours. Once, on the Saturday morning before she left, she invited me to join her. I was surprised—I didn't know her very well at all—but quickly put on my shoes to go. It seemed important, somehow.

The morning was cool. The heat hadn't set in yet, and the birds were still out. Kathy and I walked for a while without saying anything. She seemed so *sad*. I didn't know what to say. I wasn't as depressed as I was earlier that year, but I could relate to the look in her eyes and the stoop of her shoulders.

"Did you see my new tattoo?" she asked once we'd been walking twenty minutes.

"The one on your wrist? Yeah. What does it say?"

"Joy."

"Oh." It didn't seem very fitting. Joy? I didn't think she seemed very joyful.

"It's a reminder to myself."

We kept walking.

"Your mom tells me you've had a hard year," she said.

"Yeah. But it's getting better."

"I wonder what keeps you going."

When we got back to the house, I went directly to my room. I grabbed the Bible sitting on my nightstand and knelt before the bed in the traditional praying position, like the saints might have done. I opened to the middle of the text, to the Psalms.

> I will extol you, O Lord, for you have
> drawn me up
> And have not let my foes rejoice over me.

O Lord my God, I cried to you for help,
And you have healed me...
...Weeping may tarry for the night,
but joy comes with the morning.
Psalm 30

I closed the Bible slowly as assurance fell over my spirit.

I will *never* leave you nor forsake you.

I know You won't, God.

~

And yet.

Even with the reassurance from God, and with the depression lifted towards the end of that year, I was still hungry, and not just for the food I hadn't been eating. I hungered for love, from my sister Abby, a friend, a boy. It was a deep kind of longing that came from somewhere deep inside me.

I carried the brief Study Hall conversation with me for the rest of the year—the rest of high school, really—image an obsession more than ever, for myself and for all the boys to come. Somehow, God was tangled amidst those things.

Though the longing kept growing, I thought depression was gone forever, that I was finally free, that it couldn't possibly be worse than it'd been.

3

My dad finally made up his mind: we were moving to Colorado. Everything was new— the mountains to our west, the rise of Denver's skyline to the north, and the apparent lack of Bakersfield's palm trees and tumble weeds. Our new suburb was full of walking and biking trails, and the comparably milder summer weather didn't keep us stuck inside panting in front of the air-conditioner. I couldn't wait for the fall's yellow leaves and December's snow, glad to finally be out of the desert.

I was ready for the move. Freshman year had been... Well, it'd been. I was sick of hating myself. I was friendless—even Abby was gone to college—and was seeking the newness that came with change.

The only thing I knew I'd miss was our church, the one place even more familiar than my childhood home. Calvary Bible Church was the place where saggy ladies came up to me, squeezed my cheek, and told me, motioning with their bony hands, that they remembered when I was *this big*. It was the place where I'd crawled under pews to chase a bouncy ball, the place where I hid on the secret staircase between the classrooms. It was the place I'd first tasted Jesus in a bland round wafer, drunk his blood in Welch's concord grape juice.

Calvary was a place of unsaid rules. For the adults, it was no alcohol and an expectation to attend at least three times a week. For kids like me, it was a rejection of sinful music and the forbidden items—tank tops, kissing, etc. One trendy T-shirt circulating the youth group was hot pink and short-sleeved, sporting *"Modest is Hottest!"* across the chest in small, sparkly letters. Yes, I wore it.

I attended Calvary's youth group. I slunk in early and left late, tied to Abby's schedule, and was relatively unnoticed. I was quiet; I didn't say much, but I enjoyed the Sunday and Wednesday night Bible studies. I liked the rousing lessons, genuinely wanting to be a better person and to be able to embrace the humility that I thought Abby probably needed more than I.

The only person who really took notice of me at Calvary when I was a young teen was Chris, a college kid. He was large and awkward, and I think he was drawn to my shyness, not in any creepy way, but more in a kindly big-brother way. He hovered over me whenever I was sitting alone against the wall and made it a point to accept my mom's invitations to dinner at our place. When I gave up presents one year for Christmas in exchange for donations to the poor (inspired by the pastor, obviously), Chris was the one who gave me a present anyway: a huge black leather Bible with my name embossed in gold letters at the bottom.

Now, years later, I tend to scoff at the culture that I was so immersed in. It's popular nowadays to poke fun at evangelicalism. I make fun of myself to avoid my disappointment with a church that, as it turns out, had a few things that I now believe are misconstrued. A *Modest is Hottest* T-shirt? Eye roll. Six literal days in the Creation account? I don't think so, not anymore. But even though I think some things were misguided, I can't deny the positive impact the church had in my life. I scoff, but I remember it with a tender fondness.

But I liked West Bowles, our new church in Colorado, better. It was more laid-back. People wore jeans! They didn't seem to judge one another, and there wasn't an invisible set of rules we were expected to follow. The youth group didn't have any pretension. You came as you were, and if you didn't have everything together, well, whatever. At least you were there.

Instead of traditional mission trips, the group went on vacations. We drove half-way across the country in an obnoxious white van, adorned in orange flames, as kids danced in the aisle to loud pop music the entire way. At Calvary, dancing wasn't forbidden per se... just judged. The West Bowles youth group *loved* dancing.

I think the change in churches was good for me. I'd just begun to question all of Calvary's expectations, so a place like West Bowles helped me enjoy church again. Even my parents seemed to ease up on all their rules.

My health's improvement coincided with the move to Colorado. I wasn't depressed anymore. It felt like the fog in my head had finally disappeared, and I was able to see the move as an opportunity for a fresh beginning.

My faith felt stronger now that I was feeling better, my "connection" with God more correctly wired. I could think and feel normally again, which meant I could think and feel my faith again—meaning that I could "hear" God once more. It seemed that whenever my feelings were in order, so was my faith. This meant my faith tended to bounce up and down with my mood. So, for now, it was strong.

My eating habits were slowly going back to normal. My parents knew about my trouble with food, and they gave me their support, making sure to check in with me each day. They encouraged me to be open about my problem, and I was. It helped having someone to talk to about it. Like with Susan, "talk therapy" worked as a source of accountability. Not that it went away completely or forever—it didn't. For now, at least, I had a *little* relief. "Relief" seems an appropriate word for my sophomore year of high school.

My family seemed happier in Colorado. I spent my quiet life at school, my new church, or at home. Abby was away at college and so was her moody presence in the family. My mom was finally pursing a seminary career she'd wanted pre-children, something she loved but not something she'd actually end up doing as a career, and my dad decided to follow along, pursuing something he didn't know he loved yet, but something he *would* actually end up doing. At first, he wanted another master's degree only because that's what he thought God was telling him to do. He was out of his funk, also feeling better like me, which was a noticeable change. Plus, since the carrot business had sold, he was finally free financially to do something new. Later he'd become a hospital chaplain, something he felt to be his true calling. His gentle personality was suited to such a job.

I admired my parents for pursuing dreams in their forties, for pursuing things they felt God wanted them to do. They didn't just *talk* about faith. They actually lived it. I wanted to be like them, the kind of person who lived out what she believed.

But both my parents were overwhelmed, since they were starting school after not having touched a textbook in twenty-two years, and, as such, they were understandably a bit preoccupied. So, for a time, a young woman named Lilly stepped in as surrogate.

When my mom hired Lilly to help with laundry and cleaning, she was essentially hiring her to do the family dirty work. I'm sure Lilly didn't know it at the time she responded to the job post, but she would become, for the first three years of our life in Colorado, the Alice in our Brady Bunch family. Mom gave her the stuff she didn't feel like doing on a given day, like organizing a closet, making dinner, or giving the poodles a bath. Or like driving me home from school.

I was a year late to get my license—a casualty of the move from California to Colorado—so Lilly brought me home from school until I was seventeen. I thought we had so much in common, Lilly and me. A love for anything sappy, for instance. Yes, she was very old, twenty-one or something, and she was married, something I desperately wanted as a part of my own destiny, but she seemed genuinely interested in my teenage life.

She had things to say about what I was wearing,

something usually seen as insignificant in the Shane household. *Finally*, someone appreciated why I needed to get up so early to curl my hair and try on five different shirts. She even took me shopping once; I thought my life had *finally* begun. Her compliments, from my shoes to my grades at school, became expected.

Lilly never told me when I was being an idiot, which, to this day, I appreciate as quite a feat. She held a straight face when I shared one of my many angry letters to the editor of a Christian magazine. That time, I wrote about how *Twilight's* Edward and Bella were no different from Romeo and Juliet, demanding that the editorial recant its opposition to "harmful teaching." I don't remember what Lilly had to say about it, but she didn't stop me from mailing the thing. In fact, she even agreed to see the movies with me. (That's amazing and embarrassing at the same time.)

Every car ride, Lilly asked me about my day, remembering the names of my teachers, something my parents couldn't even do. It's not that my parents didn't care—they just didn't have time. I didn't let it bother me. Lilly knew when I had a test or a big paper and left me little notes saying "You can do it!" on my desk or on my pillow.

She had a quiet faith that I admired, which I thought translated in her thoughtfulness. I think she took me under her wing as someone to influence and bless. It made me want to bless others in return, and I concentrated my efforts on my younger siblings, Emma, Ian, and Elly. I started leaving them notes too, my little clichéd bits of encouragement written in Expo marker on their bathroom mirrors. I encouraged Ian to try to make friends in the new neighborhood. I helped Emma pick out her clothes at the mall and told her it was okay if she wasn't the size she wanted. I listened to Elly pluck at her guitar, telling her that she could be like Taylor Swift if she practiced enough. I wanted to be a thoughtful person, just like Lilly was, and hoped being a good sister would make me one. I wanted to make God—and Lilly—proud. (I had yet to make an effort with Abby. Even I couldn't be *that* Christian.)

I liked the way Lilly talked about God, in a way that seemed both genuine and unassuming. On our drives we talked a lot about who we thought God was, and she made Him seem kinder than I'd given Him credit for. She also helped me feel better about my body, at least for a while, just because she didn't seem self-conscious about hers.

Most importantly, Lilly always knew what boy was currently on the cute radar and cared to ask me about him, feeding my hopes and dreams. "Talking to any boys lately?" She knew a thing or two about romance. (She was *married.*)

So, when she moved, leaving Colorado, I felt like I'd lost an older sister. She was the Abby I had always wanted.

∿

Some days I felt beautiful, some days I didn't. I was a short, pretty blonde with a few pimples, nothing special, but nothing to feel bad about either. I should've been kinder to myself. I wasn't the drop-dead-gorgeous type, but I was cute enough.

I couldn't manage to see myself through God's eyes, though that was often preached at youth group. I only saw myself through my own distorted vision that often acted as an obsessed compulsion. I listened to the dark voice whispering negative insecurities into my ear.

You need to be better. You need to be better.

I longed for a boyfriend to tell me I was beautiful, but even when a boy—my friend, Jared—agreed to go with me to a Sadie's Hawkins dance, I felt let down. Here I was, not depressed anymore and with everything in life going my way, and I *still* felt dissatisfied. Would I never be complete until I had the man I wanted? If only someone would love me... *then* I could be fully happy. That's what I told God in my prayers.

You are accepted. You are redeemed.

Am I, though?

God was telling me that I was valued, that I was already loved. I didn't have to long for something else, because I had His love right in front of me. Still, I persisted in searching to fulfill my desire in a romantic relationship.

There's a misconception that Christians always manage to trust God, but that's simply not the case. Trust is a back and forth thing, a wrestling of faith. It is never easy: salvation and sanctification are not the same things.

～

By my junior year, I'd had it remarkably easy; the only real worry in my life was the amount of homework I had each night. A perfectionist, I aimed for stardom in everything I did: in my grades, in my rigorous piano lessons, and in my faith, something I would say was most important to me. I believed that if I pleased God enough, life would go my way. If things didn't go as expected, I assumed it was because I somehow wasn't as good as God wanted me to be. Was I praying enough? I prayed every day. Helping others as much as I should? I was involved in ministry. Setting an example for my younger sisters and brother? I made sure I spent one-on-one time with each of them to prove my devotion.

It was a long laundry list for Christian living. Daily prayer. Check. Helping others. Check. Being a good example. Check. Where did I pick up this way of thinking? That's not what my parents believed. That's not what they told us at church every week. That's not what Christianity is about. Christianity is about grace, not the pressing need to *do better*. Maybe it had to do more with my personality than with what I actually believed to be true.

But what I hadn't quite perfected was the boyfriend thing, which I hoped to remedy.

$\sim$

Kids at church called Andrew the "sexy, lumberjack Jesus." Dark curly hair, a thick long beard, and a six-pack that would forgive anyone's sins.

I noticed him, not only because he was tall and handsome, but because he was smart. He went to a different school than me, but I'd heard the tales of his intelligence circulating the youth group. A seventeen-year-old reading Plato? Yes, please. He was his school's beloved quarterback but supposedly held more interest in books than in being the popular kid. He had started going to my church not long before I had, so we made mutual friends. Of course, it took me a year to get enough courage to say anything but, "Hey."

I finally worked up the nerve to approach Andrew on a Sunday night after youth group. We sat inside a Mexican restaurant with a group of other kids, and I picked at my quesadilla without really eating it. I faked ease, and we talked for just a little while, about anything I thought would impress him.

"Oh, you like Steinbeck? What a coincidence, so do I." (I *tried* reading *Grapes of Wrath* in the fifth grade.) "I'll definitely try *East of Eden*."

"You like to hike? I hike all the time." (That wasn't exactly true.)

"Maybe I'll come to one of your games. I like football." (Also a lie.)

I left our conversation quite pleased with myself. Now he thought I was smart *and* athletic.

My friend, Lewis, stopped me on the way to my car to tell me that Andrew and I were *perfect* for each other. I shook my head adamantly, assuring him that he was overreacting. It was just a conversation, nothing more.

On the way home, I called my mom and told her I'd met the man of my dreams.

~

I read Andrew's *East of Eden* in two days, forcing myself to like it even though I didn't really understand the novel's concept of *thou mayest*. What did *thou mayest*—God's gift of allowing us to make our own choices in life—have to do with me and my list of to-do's? Nothing. For me, it wasn't "thou mayest" but "thou must."

I planned to talk to him about the book during the backpacking trip the following weekend. Honestly, I hadn't planned on going backpacking until I learned Andrew was. I wasn't really the backpacking type, didn't even know what it entailed, but I didn't think it could be that hard.

Except the hike was excruciatingly difficult. I was one of the last to arrive at camp, with blisters covering my heels and even bigger blisters on my shoulders where my pack had dug through my shirt and into my skin. My hair was sticky with sweat, and my face was burnt bright red from the lack of sunscreen. I clumsily dropped my back-pack and sank into someone's folding chair, too exhausted to set up a tent or pump filtered water into my bottle down by the stream. I couldn't bring myself even to look at Andrew, who'd apparently run the entire way. I bet he didn't even have any blisters.

The next day, everyone decided to go bouldering.

"What's bouldering?" I asked one of the girls. She looked like all the other girls on the trip, adorned in feather earrings, plaid, and Teva sandals.

"Rock climbing without ropes. Jumping and stuff. It's a Colorado thing."

"Ah." I wondered if it was too late to fake a headache.

I will never forget bouldering. Flinging myself onto giant rocks, scraping the skin right off my hands. Rolling down the side of another rock, landing on my stomach. Climbing up what I thought was a mountain with my eyes closed, too afraid to look up or down. My fingernails clung to crevices when my sweaty hands made gripping the rock wall impossible. I truly thought I was going to die that day, I really did, but I would only return with bruises, scrapes, and ripped-up fingers.

I told myself that Andrew might be looking, might admire my participation. Every jump and every fall (I was an inexperienced climber), he saw. Analyzed. Every ounce of my effort was noted. Even when I needed a hand to climb one of the bigger rocks, he saw that I was at least trying. I could feel his eyes on me—I *wanted* to feel his eyes on me. Was he looking? No, but I would perform just in case.

I was very aware of his presence—where he was, whom he was talking to—even though I tried to keep myself from looking at him.

When I fell yet again, *hard,* I hoped he wasn't looking after all. I lay there, on my back, willing the tears not to come. Someone came over and asked me if I was okay, and I said I was, just needed a minute. I told them to go on ahead of me. (Let me cry in peace!) I wanted to seem strong. Instead, I was the weakest of the group, clearly the most pathetic.

My entire body ached on the day we hiked back to where the vans were parked. I hadn't talked to Andrew at all in three days; I pretty much avoided all eye contact, though I had imagined his eyes on me when everyone sat around the firepit with our baked beans and hot choco-late. He didn't talk to me either. I decided that I needed to be one of the first to get back to the vans. Maybe that would win me his favor. It wasn't a race, but I needed to win. I needed him to notice me doing something right.

Andrew ran the way back, so I did too, a little way behind him. I ran, with my now mostly empty pack banging up and down on my bandaged shoulders, feet screaming at me. Sweat dripped and burned my eyes; the muscles in my calves moaned complaints that I forced myself to ignore. Adrenaline filled my chest as I passed by the other girls, boys even.

I don't know how I did it. I was completely out of shape. I was utterly exhausted, covered in Band-Aids. The thought of his approval drove me past the others, up and down the winding trail, and, finally, back to the vans. I was the first girl back. The gold medalist, Miss Colorado herself.

Andrew was slumped against a tree, asleep, and didn't wake until everyone else arrived.

～

I think Lewis was the one who invited Andrew to hot tub, and he showed up one night without my asking.

I wanted the hot tubbing to become a ritual in our small friend group, even though it happened inconsis-tently. I never questioned why they never invited me over to *their* homes. I simply waited around my cell phone on Fridays, hoping they'd text me, asking for an invite. Why *didn't* they invite me over? For all I cared about them, they should have.

My mom liked the guys to come over to our house in lieu of me going to someone else's. This way, she knew what was going on, got to know the boys I was hanging out with. She trusted me and wanted to trust them too.

I think it gave her a sense of involvement. The guys would spend at least twenty minutes chatting with her over a bowl of their favorite sour cherry drops or home-made candy before changing into their suits, fully aware that my parents would make their presence known by occasionally checking in on us. It was fine that the guys were practically all half-naked, just so long as I wasn't in a too-skimpy bikini. (They didn't insist upon a one-piece because we no longer went to church at Calvary. Even the leaders at the West Bowles youth group wore bikinis.) They trusted me to keep the gatherings chaste.

I usually sat across from Andrew, loving every time he talked to me. In reality, I didn't speak with him all that much. But, when I did, every word was carefully chosen: "Yesterday, when I was working out, like I usually do..."

As the backpacking trip proved, Andrew was one of the many muscled boys at the church. He was a prom-inent leader in their little Cross-fit community. And just as there was an enormous amount of facial hair in that small church sample size, there was also an abnormal number of six-packs, all stomachs shown off when they came over to hot tub. I don't know what it was—maybe it was something in the water, maybe it was some sort of secret bodybuilding club.

I was never an athletic person, but my obsession with

exercise began quickly. I started weight-lifting with a trainer. I started hiking and running with my dad on weekends. My fixation on being skinny changed to a fixation on being fit. Push-ups before bed, squats in the shower. I wanted to drop in hints during our conversations, hints that I, too, knew what a bench press was. I learned to say, "I just want to be healthy" any time my parents questioned my new obsession. "Healthy" no longer meant balance or "everything in moderation" as it once had. "Healthy" was no longer unique to the individual. Healthy was synonymous with svelte legs, kale salads, chiseled stomachs, low sugar, sculpted shoulders, and being girlfriend material.

My exercise obsession was too extreme to be normal. I went about it frantically, mind racing every time I went downstairs to my parent's basement gym. I saw myself differently in the mirror than I actually was in real life. My eyes only saw my stomach, the *only* place I carried weight, instead of the rest of my thin body. I didn't technically have an eating disorder, not in the medical sense, but my eating was certainly disordered. I worshiped God, but I also worshiped my body and how I wanted it to look. I should've gone to counseling again, but I kept the obsession to myself. After all, I was just being "healthy."

Besides his exercise regimen, Andrew often talked about the books he was reading. Books I'd never heard of or bothered to read, classics I'd bought but left untouched. I wanted to be the kind of person who read classic literature, but I wasn't. I decided I needed to boost my intellect. One Saturday morning, I brought a cardboard box up to my room and started sorting through the novels on my shelf, stacking all the sappy Christian romances into storage. Goodbye, *Love on the Open Prairie*, and hello, Hemingway. This would be a new era, when I pretended to like books that I didn't.

I became very good at molding myself to be what I thought Andrew wanted. What if Andrew hadn't been around? Would I be any different? I'd probably be molding myself to someone else. For too many years, I hated myself when I didn't work out. I even still feel the imaginary pressure to be literary—whatever that is. Those things have just become a part of me, unquestioned and harmless. (Is it harmless?)

This molding is interesting, because I was trying to do the exact same thing in my faith. I was taught that being "Christ-like" was a part of spiritual growth, that "becoming more and more like Jesus" was a sign of spiritual maturity. I was very aware of my actions—Was I loving? Was I kind?—at school and at home because I desperately wanted to be like Jesus, certain that that was what God wanted for me.

If I hadn't been so obsessed with Andrew, I may have been able to better focus on my character. My distraction kept my mind busy, and I don't think I was as devoted to God as I thought I was. I still had that ache deep inside of me, that longing for love, and I persisted in thinking it would come from a boy.

$\sim$

Oddly enough, my love for Andrew was the thing that brought my mom and me closer together.

Until I was about sixteen, my mom and I used to argue a lot about a lot of things, all unimportant, like the length of my uniform skirt. We were too alike: stubborn and convinced our way was the best—and only—way. But as I got older, other parts of our alikeness brought camaraderie instead of an argument. We liked to organize. We liked to entertain. We liked the same movies. We were both romantics.

Mom did struggle with body image, though. She didn't mean to set a bad example; that was never her intention. Weight was her personal demon, and I think it just hopped from her shoulder onto my own without her knowing. Even when she came to finally accept and love herself during her time in seminary, I still bore the weight of my own insecurity.

After my mom got more settled into life and classes at the seminary, we spent more time together. We spent many hours on her bed, watching BBC dramas and analyzing any hot tub conversations. Andrew was a common topic of conversation. My mom analyzed only what I told her, all positive aspects—nothing which would have given her a clue that he wasn't interested. So, she hoped on my behalf, just as much as I did. Honestly, I don't think she meant to set me up for disappointment. Andrew was simply a talking point, a means to share something with her daughter. Andrew was something we didn't have to argue about. Talking about Andrew meant I was talking to her, spending time with her, confiding in her. What mom wouldn't want that? She egged me on, yeah, but maybe she did so just to feel like a part of my life.

"Did he talk to you? What did he say? What did you say? What do you think it meant?"

~

"So, you reading any good books lately?" I asked Andrew. This was now my go-to question. Books were safe. I wanted to tell him all about the new workouts I was doing, but I was afraid I didn't look the part. No matter how hard I tried, my stomach remained soft and my arms weak. I could talk to him about faith—we had that in common at least—but I didn't want to come across as *too* spiritual. (I mean, I *was* a spiritual person—I thought my life centered around my beliefs—but I also didn't want to come across as preachy or... not cool. Cool, as a teenager, is important too.)

The guys and I were sitting in my basement after two hours in the hot tub. One boy was sitting against the wall, trying to see how far he could fling cards from his deck. The diamonds, he claimed, went the farthest. The others were looking at something on one of their phones, which left Andrew and me with nothing to do but stare at the wall or at each other. It felt natural talking to the others, but with Andrew? My tongue couldn't find the words. Neither could his, apparently.

"No, not really. Just books for school," he said.

I waited for him to ask me the same question, but he didn't. I liked that he was quiet—it made him more mysterious—but it made it hard for me to talk to him. I fiddled with my wet braid, squeezing the excess water from the end and onto the carpet. My hair smelled of chlorine, even though I'd rinsed it out.

I knew that he'd decided to do track that spring. I knew that he was working for a piano-moving company. I knew that he read Faulkner. (Who was that?) What I didn't know was how to talk to him about any of it.

Finally, he asked, "How about you?"

"*Great Expectations.*" My answer came quickly. Planned.

"Oh, cool. I love his characterization of Miss Havisham."

"Me too." I smiled. This was good. This was definite progress in our relationship.

I wanted to ask him if he was going to prom or not. If he was going to ask someone. But how to phrase it? I'd agonized over the question the night before, trying to come up with the perfect syntax.

"Are you asking anyone to prom?" Or maybe, "*Do you think* you'll ask anyone to prom?" I could go with, "I'm thinking about whether or not I'll go to prom," and just wait to see what he'd say, but that seemed risky.

I didn't end up saying any of it. Only asked if he wanted water. He did.

I wish I could go back in time, take my younger self by the shoulders, and shake the passivity and the daydreams right out of her. The thought of her, just waiting around in her mind palace until a boy deigned to show any interest, troubles me. I'm a naturally driven person—what was holding me back from just going after something I wanted? Was I so concentrated on being someone I wasn't that I lost track of who I really was? When would I get myself back?

I thought about Miss Havisham later that night. I was in bed with the light already off, going between my thoughts and my nightly prayers. I thought Miss Havisham's story was simply too sad. The way she kept on hoping and longing for love resonated with me, and I was angry with Dickens for not being kinder. My greatest fear? *Being alone forever.* All those romance books made that seem like the worst possible fate.

"So... God..." I went from Miss Havisham to my prayer.

"I really like him, and... *please?*" It seemed like all I ever prayed about was that stupid boy.

You are never alone, for I am with you. I will never fail you.

The Tuesday night before his school's dance, I was frustrated to see Andrew wasn't at youth group. This would be the last opportunity for him to ask me. I waited anxiously, looking at my watch inconspicuously during the pastor's talk. But then it hit me: He wasn't there because he was probably at *that very moment* decorating my car with balloons and "Prom?" signs and just waiting for me to come outside.

He wasn't. He wasn't there, waiting for me. Wanting me.

As I drove home, I struggled with my dismay. Why didn't he see that I was worth asking? Maybe he didn't like my pooch stomach and I needed to exercise more, or maybe I needed to read more so that I seemed more interesting. I needed to be exactly what he wanted. I needed to try harder.

"Please, God? Just let him ask me." I liked praying in my car. It was a quiet space for me to vent, to hear my own voice against the quiet. "I know it's stupid. But, God, please? Please understand."

I fell silent, punched on the radio.

Scripture taught that I was supposed to "wait on the Lord." *I wait on the Lord, more than watchmen wait for the morning.* But what did that even mean? That concept seemed so vague. Being a watchman seemed like an awfully boring job. And, besides, I was tired of waiting.

"Why isn't God answering my prayer? I don't hear His voice." I asked my mom that evening. I had my head in her lap, and she ran her fingers through my hair.

"Is He not answering, or are you not listening?"

"I just don't get it. He knows how much I want this."

"He does."

"Mom, I have this desire. I want love—is that so bad? It's inside of me, and I can't get rid of it."

"I don't know if having Andrew will make that feeling go away. But I get it." Her finger caught in a tangle, and she tugged at it gently.

"Why don't you ask him to *your* prom?" my mom asked. "We bought that nice dress months ago. Otherwise, it's just going to hang there."

～

I'm walking through mirrored halls, weeping. Strange sobs come from my mouth, the sound of sorrow.

I see myself in the mirrors. My skin is sagging around my neck, and wrinkles line the sides of my face. My arms are white and flabby, all trace of muscle replaced by thick layers of fat. Is that really me? I am decaying before my very eyes.

I am wearing a long, beaded gown. The prom dress. The pink is faded, and sequins fall to the floor as I walk, making a tinkling sound as they do. The rips in the fabric grow larger, and I leave a trail of sequins.

I am Miss Havisham.

It was my dream that made me decide to ask Andrew to my school's prom. I couldn't bear the thought of being the Dickens character, forever plagued with regret. Miss Havisham never found love. She wasn't good enough for the man, so she stayed in her rotting wedding dress, caught in her delusions, forever hoping. I didn't want to rot.

≈

I wanted to seem nonchalant when I asked Andrew to the dance, so of course I agonized about how to accomplish just that. It needed to look like an afterthought, lest I look desperate. I decided to approach him after youth group, at that Mexican restaurant, where my friends and I went for our weekly burritos after church.

"So... Andrew." This was as good a time as any. We were still standing in line to order.

"What's up?"

I told him that I'd had a *random* thought the other day about my school's dance. Just an afterthought, of sorts.

"Yeah?" He knew exactly where I was going with this.

"I need a date, and I thought you'd maybe want to go with me. Just as friends, or whatever."

"*This* Saturday?"

"Yeah. But if you're busy, you know, it's no big deal. At all."

"No, no. I can go."

"Really?" Success.

Since my parents were out of town the weekend of the dance, I got ready on my own. I felt beautiful when I was finished putting on my pink sequined dress. I looked like a woman. Well, more like Barbie. A Barbie-woman. There were layers of makeup and hairspray and perfume and, of course, the Spanx. Although I liked the way the dress's neckline plunged to my non-existent cleavage and clung to my hips, I was preoccupied with making sure the Spanx didn't creep up to the open back. I definitely didn't need to wear Spanx—I had no rolls to worry about yet— but I worried nonetheless.

I was ready three hours early, and Andrew was an hour late.

I spent my waiting changing in and out of the Spanx. About every twenty minutes, I wriggled out of the nude compression shorts to take a few deep breaths before squeezing into them again. I knew I wanted a flat stom- ach; I wanted to look sleek. They were so uncomfortable! I debated taking them off, but Andrew arrived before I made up my mind.

He looked nice, even though his suit looked like it'd never been ironed. His pink tie matched my dress by accident. He handed me a small plastic container.

"Oh, wow. You didn't have to." I slipped on the corsage and tossed the box on the bench by the door as we walked out.

His small car smelled like a locker room. A large lacrosse stick in the backseat protruded into the front seat, right between us. To see Andrew, I had to peer around the net.

"Sorry about the mess," he said, gesturing to the loose papers, paper cups, and stale pieces of popcorn at my heeled feet.

"It's fine." I fingered the corsage band where the white rose had already gotten loose and fallen off my wrist.

Our prom was held at Hudson Gardens, a cabin-like event center. Someone had fixed Technicolor disco balls to the wood beamed ceiling, ruining the rustic-like feel. It was much too small; we had to push through people to get across the room. Because there were so many of us, the room felt hot and stuffy. I surreptitiously dabbed my armpits with a tissue.

The dance itself was agonizing. I stood beside one of the raised punch tables, leaving to fill and refill my plastic cup while Andrew stood on the other side of the table, looking at his own untouched cup. I thought he might be looking at me, but every time I glanced over, he was still staring into his punch. *Look at me. Look at me. Look at me. God, let him look at me.*

"Another slow one," he murmured as a new song

started. "The DJ could at least mix it up a little, you'd think."

We looked at the couples out on the floor, bodies pressed close together. I didn't want to be the one to suggest we go out there. I wanted him to do that. So, we just stood there, song after song, watching, like we were at a fancy ballet instead of a high school dance.

This was what I wanted, wasn't it? Wasn't this what'd I been longing for? I'd been waiting for this night, but it just felt weird. The fantasy wasn't going as I imagined. All I ever wanted was a date with Andrew, and now it felt lacking.

Finally, the songs progressed in tempo and the slow dancing turned into jumping, dancing, a style circa 2010. I thought this would be better, but I suddenly became embarrassed, unwilling to let go of any inhibition. You *had* to let go of inhibition for this kind of dancing, because you were guaranteed to look like an idiot. I couldn't do that in front of Andrew, and I wasn't sure if I could even pretend to be silly. I was too aware of myself.

And how was I supposed to dance to pop music in Spanx? I could move from side to side, but there was no way I could jump up and down, not when I could barely breathe. I excused myself to go to the bathroom. I needed to get out of the Spanx for just a few minutes.

On my way, someone told me that I was leaving sequins on the floor behind me.

$\sim$

I *finally* got the hint when he stopped answering my texts the days following prom. First, it was that he was busy with a new job and couldn't hang out. Then, it was just no answer.

The guy was trying to be nice about it. Didn't want to lead me on. It just took me a while to understand and give up the daydream. I was a little dense, but I wasn't stupid.

The last-ditch effort was the movie. We'd joked earlier that year about *Pride & Prejudice*, how it was my favorite movie and his least. (And the fact that it was somewhat literary, I thought, could win me points.) I insisted that he give it another chance and invited him over to watch it on a Friday when he didn't have work.

I spent the morning tidying the house. I wanted to set the tone for that afternoon, as if a clean countertop or fluffed pillows would make for a great cinematic experience. I vacuumed and folded blankets, wiped down the coffee table and organized the stack of catalogues. I made peanut butter cookies and made sure they came out of the oven right at 4:00 p.m. so that the smell would linger.

He didn't show. When I called him, he said he was out of town with his dad on some business trip, the movie—and me—completely forgotten.

I went to my room, kicked a pillow across the floor, and lay on the bed, staring at the ceiling fan that went around in lazy taunting circles.

Okay, so he didn't like me. What was wrong with me? Was I not fit enough? Didn't read enough? Didn't hike enough?

You are not enough. That voice, again. Not God's.

And why wasn't God answering my prayer? It may've been petty, but my pain *was* real. God was silent to my hurt, and I couldn't understand it. Was I just not listening?

I knew faith was more than just getting what I wanted from God. It was more than just whining about my woes. I knew that. But because I wanted Andrew so deeply, because the desire for love kept growing and growing the older I got, I began to question whether God even cared. This shouldn't have rocked me so much—God was a consistent and steady presence in my life, after all—but it bothered me enough to make me feel uneasy. For the first time in my life, I tasted doubt. What did this mean about my faith? If this was happening now, with my simple hurt feelings, what would doubt look like in my future?

4

I went to Africa on a missions trip the summer before my senior year. When I came back, my faith was anything but strong. While all the other kids on my team left Africa feeling like little white heroes, so "connected to God" because they'd given up clean sheets for two and a half weeks, I left Kenya and Uganda feeling completely hollow.

I'd been out of the country on vacations before, when I was younger—China, France, Mexico—but the trip to Africa was different. Uncomfortable.

My group's five chaperones were busy trying to make sure our group was on time and on the right bus schedule. Debriefing the day's events wasn't really their strong suit. My parents weren't with me to whisper interpretations into my ear; I was on my own to decipher what I was seeing. I didn't appreciate the culture when I should have. I saw only differences between my home and theirs. Especially the differences that didn't seem fair.

In Kenya, we visited a couple different orphanages,

churches, and local Kampala ministries. Honestly, it felt like a poverty tour for the "white rich kids league of America." *Look, kids! The poor!* I recognize the white superiority and missionary complex now, but I also think I recognized it then, though I couldn't define what it was. It's not that I am against mission trips. The intention behind the trip was good, which shouldn't necessarily be discounted. Yet something just didn't feel right. Plus, I was so caught up in the differences between my culture and theirs that I failed to appreciate any of the country's uniqueness and heritage. All I saw was sadness. I wish I'd understood that just because a country is different, it doesn't make it inherently bad.

I remember standing in a too-small cement room of an orphanage, handing out a crayon to each little hand outstretched my way. All of the children wore red and white checkered uniforms and sandals that didn't cover their dusty feet. After a meal of rice and chicken broth, they pulled and tugged at my clothes and arms: *play with us, play with us.* I can't remember their faces, but I remember how it bothered me when they rubbed their snotty noses into my long prairie skirt. My peers pulled out their cell phones to take selfies with the littlest ones, hoping for the perfect picture to post on Facebook upon the return home. A picture to remember how we'd changed their lives forever with a few coloring books. I left the orphanage ashamed that I was concerned about the smell lingering on my skin.

I remember standing against the wall of a humid, dark room, staring at the women sorting peanuts on a floor covered in shells. They wore large colorful scarves twisted around their heads and thick waists. The room was hot and stuffy; all I wanted to do was leave and go outside, to breathe fresh air. I felt faint and tried to nurse my warm water bottle slowly.

"They all have AIDS," one of the chaperones said. "They make peanut butter to support their families."

"Is it, like, contagious?" the girl next to me asked.

"We should totally help them. Give them money or something," another girl said.

"They're dying?" I asked the chaperone.

"Yeah. And any medication is expensive."

I opened my mouth to say something, but words didn't come. This was just too unfair. If I were sick, my parents would drop everything and spend whatever it cost to take care of me. These women deserved treatment, and I felt powerless to help them.

I remember lining my nostrils with Vicks VapoRub to help block the smell radiating through Kenya's largest slum. I couldn't believe I was actually in a slum—it seemed surreal, like something you read about but don't actually suppose exists. I was in shock—I couldn't think.

Shanty houses, with slanted metal roofs and sides with broken wood doors, lined the streets. Most people were sitting or walking outside their homes, some scowling at us and others waving, but there was one woman who looked from her window with no expression at all. She just stared blankly at me, and I froze, not sure if it was appropriate to smile. I stared back.

I looked down at my feet as I walked through the slum, one of the largest in the world, realizing that I wasn't walking on a road at all, but a packed-down layer of trash. Trash on trash on trash. Barefoot children played in the dark brown streams that flowed through the area, water full of human waste and even more trash. That's what got me—not the children's faces—the trash. No matter how much someone tried to clean, to help, there were just too many layers of both the trash and the situation. It was too complicated, too heavy, too much. What did I know about this kind of thing? Nothing. I knew nothing. I didn't know how to help or even if it was my business in the first place. I didn't know what to think. I didn't know what to feel.

By the end of our walk, I couldn't even bring myself to look at the women and men, the ones who lived there day in and day out, walking past us. How could I, when I would soon be returning to my long showers and steak and potatoes? I felt ashamed that I'd be returning home, ashamed that I thought myself above this, ashamed that I never ever wanted to come back.

"God is here. I can feel it," one of the kids said as we made our way out. I wanted to slap him. Yell at him. Something. How dare he say something like that. Of course, he could "feel" God—*he* wasn't the one living in a slum. What about the people who did live there? Did they feel God? The slum affronted my belief in God's omnipresence.

I remember Livingston, one the men we met in Uganda, squatting over our campfire as he told his story of escaping the Rwandan genocide. The sky was black, but the air was still hot. I sat a few feet away from the fire and watched his shadowed face from the other side of the flames. Livingston talked slowly, his tragic story unraveling over the hour. He said his entire family was slaughtered.

"How do you know God is good?" one of my teachers, a chaperone, asked us another night. We were again sitting around a fire, though this time the air was cooler, with Livingston and a few of the other locals, and the night's stars inspired reflective conversation.

Each kid answered the question, one by one. God was good because of their family. God was good because He always provided. Because of His constant protection.

My eyes slid over to Livingston. What would he say? He had none of those things.

"What about you, Anna?"

I looked up. "I don't know." That's all I could say.

They looked disappointed but moved on. "And you, Livingston?"

The tall, thin man paused, stood, and stared away from the fire and into the darkness. For a moment, I thought he wasn't going to answer at all. Then he turned around, and his large eyes swept over our group, over the Americans who would never truly comprehend his story.

"God is good," he finally said, slowly. "All of the time." A slight pause. "All of the time. God is good. Because that is His nature." He sat back down.

I will never, ever, forget those words. They made me wonder if, after Africa, I believed the same thing anymore. I was a young girl with her naivety crushed. I came from a prosperous family, a prosperous country, and I needed to decide how seeing destitution was going to affect my faith. I didn't know yet.

Faced with immense poverty for the first time—a first

encounter with my hopelessness—I became angry. Africa taught me that I'd equated God's goodness with happiness, something I'd chastised others for doing. Sure, I'd give up a month's allowance to donate to the women with AIDS, but it did little to make me feel better.

How could my God of love, of caring, the one I knew, exist? God is good, all of the time, because that is His nature? How could Livingston mean what he said? I'd never met a man so sincere, but it seemed incredible he could believe that.

When I think back to that experience now, I just wish that I'd been better able to process what I'd experienced. I've had time to think about my crushed naivety, but that trip still remains a dark memory. Now, I *do* trust that God is good, but I also understand why I was so shaken.

I didn't even know if I believed anymore. If God wasn't good, He wasn't the God I knew, the God I prayed to. So maybe I'd just give it all up. This would mean, in a way, that I'd be losing myself. God was so much a part of my life, that if I lost Him, I'd lose everything I knew about myself. My identity was at risk.

～

I *'m coming for you.*
    I was sitting in bed, staring at the flickering figure in front of me. He—she?—had no face, no detail. It was just a gray outline of a person, standing across the room.

It was my last morning in Africa, and the rest of the group had gone to a wildlife park. I'd gotten heatstroke the day before—we'd been handing out food in the hot sun, and I'd forgotten my water bottle—and had contracted some sort of fever during the night. I was either sleeping fitfully or throwing up in the toilet. I was drenched in sweat and so were my sheets.

But now, someone, something, was in my room, threatening me.

I'm coming for you. Just you wait and see. It was said slowly, loudly.

Was this real? Was I awake? I pinched myself, hard. Yes, I was awake. What did this thing want with me? Why was it here?

"Go away," I said aloud.

It didn't move.

"Oh God. God, help." The words just came out of me.

The figure disappeared before my very eyes.

I didn't tell anyone about that experience for a very long time, afraid they would never believe me. This wasn't some "heart of darkness" thing—the vision had little to do with my being in Africa and more to do with my vulnerable state of mind. It seemed crazy. Was I crazy? It was some sort of hallucination, I think. A side effect of the dehydration?

Yet there was something real in that hallucination that I can't really explain. Who—what—was coming for me?

~

"God?" I asked the ceiling. No. I couldn't. What if He wasn't there?

It was late; I was home from Africa. I'd gone to bed

hours earlier but couldn't fall asleep. Tonight, the darkness in my room scared me a little. I wasn't usually afraid of the dark. That seemed juvenile. But I couldn't help but feel alone. Maybe my parents would know what to do to help me.

I left my bed, went down the hall and into their room. They were asleep, of course, and I had to whisper several times before they woke and turned on a lamp.

"What's wrong?" Mom sat up.

I realized I was crying.

"Anna, what is it?"

"I don't know what it means if God isn't real." I was sobbing. "I don't know who I am."

"Is this about Africa?" Dad asked.

"I don't know what to do if I can't talk to Him. I *always* talk to Him."

"It's all right if you can't make sense of things. There are some things that we will never understand. We have to be okay with that." Mom patted the side of the bed, motioning for me to come and sit down. "Doubt is perfectly normal. Dad and I have doubted a lot, you know. We've had some really terrible things happen in our life, and doubt inevitably comes. But we get through it."

"Terrible things, like with Dad's depression?"

"And my mania, when we lived in China," Dad said.

I wiped at the tears with the back of my hand. They *never* talked about that part of his bipolar disorder. I didn't even know he *had* the bipolar disorder until recently—I thought it was just depression. Bipolar: a mood disorder that swung him high or low if he was not medicated. Since I didn't understand much about what bipolar disorder entailed, I didn't think about it much—not even when they told me about it for the first time. He hadn't had a manic episode since before I could remember, so they never needed to tell me about it. Just that it was a bad time in their life.

"Take the time to doubt," Dad said. "God will be here when you get back."

~

During the first few weeks of the school year, I began doing a little research. Through a few books from the library and browsing online, I discovered Buddhism, Hinduism, and Islam. Later, I spent hours talking to a guy on the Mormon hotline. I was curious about the different understandings of God, but I was looking for something to help me understand what I'd seen in Africa, and I couldn't find it. All belief systems had interesting values, but I couldn't reconcile them with the God I'd already personally known as the Christian God. I even dabbled with atheism, but it scared me too much to really try. I craved fairness, but couldn't find it anywhere.

It was an intellectual approach, and it wasn't going to be enough. I wasn't going to find God—or not find Him —that way.

~

I met my friend Jack after I got back from Africa, when he shared his testimony, a story of his faith, at church. Actually, I'd known him longer than that, but I didn't really get to know him until my last year of high school.

In his testimony, he said he had met Jesus. I actually flinched. *Met Jesus.* Sounded like the Sunday school cliché, "too religious." But Jack seemed so sincere.

The fact that he came from a very different background from my own piqued my interest. He wasn't like me; he was from a non-practicing Jewish family and wasn't so saturated in church that he was sick of it. He was an "outsider," and he found value in the faith I wasn't sure I understood anymore.

He was short, but he was also huge: 100% muscle. Large veins danced down his thick olive arms, and he looked like he was flexing even when he wasn't. His dark brown hair alternated from being cropped close to grown out curly and long. Jack was, per usual of our church youth group boys, attractive. I shouldn't have been surprised.

I was glad when he started coming over to hot tub at my place with Andrew and some of the other guys. He was easy to talk to—funny, and kind. He started coming over to work out on a few weekends at my place and joined in on several group hikes. I told myself I wasn't going to fall for him—not after Andrew—and since he had a girlfriend, someone I actually liked, it'd be easy enough.

I liked hearing him talk about Christianity. It sounded fresh coming from him, new and untainted. He had so many questions, and everyone else looked to me, the one at the Christian school, to answer them. I felt like a hypocrite as I explained things I now doubted.

"Man. I just think it's so cool that God knows *each* of us, you know? That He cares that much?" Jack said. He and I were sitting on the couch in my basement after the rest of the guys had left. He paged through one of the many books I'd just handed him. He wanted to know as much about church doctrine as possible, and I offered him an entire library.

"You've read all of these?" He waved a C.S. Lewis book at my face.

I eyed the large stack crowded into his arms. "Yep."

"So, you like them?"

"Yep." Hopefully the books would help him. *They certainly wouldn't help me*, I thought. I could read and read, but no amount of research was going to give me clarity. I knew the answers. I just didn't *feel* them. I wanted to feel.

∼

I couldn't go to sleep. It was one of those nights where I went from my side to my stomach and then to my other side, flipping the pillow over and over again for coolness. Eventually, I ended up on my back, staring at the plastic stars on the ceiling that clung to their dull yellow glow. I'd been having a lot of restless nights ever since Africa, wrestling with doubt.

I started to pray and then stopped, remembering that I didn't know if I wanted to do that anymore. Yeah, I *wanted* to pray, but what to say? The silence was unsettling, uncomfortable. Was my doubt damning?

Okay, maybe I did believe after all, deep down—for how could I abandon Him after all this time? I *knew* God was there. And He was good, somehow. I just knew. I couldn't lie to myself, even if it seemed somehow mature to do that. Atheism seemed grown up and sophisticated, but I couldn't quite get myself there. *Nothingness* hinted at *meaninglessness*. I was seventeen; I couldn't handle that.

So, what was I supposed to do when belief and doubt existed simultaneously?

I rolled back onto my stomach and willed Jack's face to fill my sleepless thoughts.

~

With all the time we spent together over the next few months, the crush was inevitable.

Even though he had a girlfriend.

Even though he showed no interest in me whatsoever.

Jack was kind and a good listener, cute and approachable. I fell for him easily.

It was pretty standard, to be honest, almost too similar to Andrew. Savoring every text message, overanalyzing every conversation, and daydreaming about the day he'd profess his love for me. I compared myself to the girlfriend, of course, hating how nice she was, how thin she was. Nothing new.

My mom encouraged me to get over Jack ("He *has* a *girlfriend,* Anna") and to start thinking more about college. We were lying in her bed again, in front of the

TV, flipping through channels until we found the home design network. A kitchen remodel.

"There will be plenty of guys in the future," she said, "and I don't want you to get hurt again."

"I like that one." I pointed to the screen, where an overdressed contractor installed white granite countertops.

"Did you hear what I said? There's a lot ahead of you. You have no idea what God has in store." She sounded like a mom.

"Do you like white granite?"

"Anna, are you hearing me? I feel like you're not hearing me."

"*Yes,* Mom. I get it." I couldn't see what could possibly be better than Jack.

∾

I was devastated when Jack told me he was leaving the country, off to see some random relatives since he was graduating early and had time to spare. He was excited to leave for South Africa; he'd never left the country before.

"Only two months," he said.

Only? By the time he got back, the school year would be over, and we'd be going off to different universities.

"You might see things in a different country that are, you know, hard to swallow," I told Jack as we talked about his upcoming travel, "And it's okay to be uncomfortable."

"What do you mean? I believe. Nothing will change that." He was confident in his new faith. He'd become a

Christian through a supernatural experience, and it was too fresh to question.

"Oh, I know you do. I'm just saying that it could be hard. But it's okay if it shakes you. I think I'm learning that. Slowly."

"Nothing will shake me."

"Okay, well. Good."

I hated the thought of Jack forgetting about me. I decided to give him a little something to show I cared, and, in a roundabout way, ask if he cared too. I couldn't be too forward, because he was still dating the girlfriend, but his leaving felt like he was breaking up with *me*.

I bought a journal, one of those nice leatherbound kinds with embossed edges, and filled it with travel-inspiration quotes and pictures. On the inside cover, I wrote him a long note that basically said "I love you" without actually saying it.

"I'll miss you. I'll pray for you. I'll think of you often."

Give me Jack. It was a reluctant prayer for my car rides. It was the first prayer in weeks. *Give me Jack, and I'll be completely yours.*

I gave the journal to Jack on a Tuesday, at youth group, before he left.

"It's nothing much, just a little something," I said. "No big deal."

He texted me on my drive home: "Anna, I think you need to guard your heart."

I immediately started crying, as if the emotion was just stalling, waiting around to be beckoned. My car swerved into the left lane, and I jerked the wheel to the right as an oncoming car honked its warning. I pulled over to cry.

Guard your heart? What was that supposed to mean?

I knew what it meant. Basic Christian lingo for: "Get over it." Jack was catching onto Christian jargon remarkably fast.

I felt everything at once. The sting of rejection. The embarrassment of reading into things *again*. And the terrible feeling of loneliness that overshadowed it all.

That night I didn't pray.

It wasn't because I doubted God's existence, not really. I'd question Christianity a thousand times, but for now, the doubt was gone. It was okay to doubt, just like my parents said. I knew this now, and I had a sense of security about it. I could pray if I wanted to.

Not that what I experienced in Africa doesn't still haunt me—it does. I still see those dying women sorting peanuts. I still see the children running barefoot in that trash. It still doesn't make sense to me. But I think God is, somehow, in things that don't make sense, though I didn't understand that then.

❧

I know how Jack must have felt when he was giving his testimony. He probably feared others' judgment, knowing that most people wouldn't really believe him. It's crazy, this "meeting Jesus." Can one explain something supernatural? Something *other*?

The dream is at first clunky and may appear over the

top, like so many dreams. But then it becomes so vivid, so clear, so understood.

I'm standing on a grand underground stage, in front of everyone I know. I am to receive "a great burden," something vague that everyone in the dream apparently understands, including myself. The "burden" is something I know I deserve, something I know to be inevitable. I've done something terrible, and the burden is my punishment.

It happens. The burden is a weight that falls over me, crushing me to nothing. It is a sound, so loud and powerful that it fills my entire body until it implodes. It is desire—a desperate, colorful, agonizing *longing*— so strong that my heart cracks in two. I shatter.

Once I cease to be, my spirit—it's a feeling more than anything—walks down the stage and through a kind of door. The door is too heavy for me to open—I can't open it on my own. Someone opens it for me.

And then I'm with Him—*Him*—walking in greens and blues. His face is vague, but I know it anyway, know He is smiling. My body is there, but it isn't. We walk, and I giggle like a little child. The happiness tastes funny. It is *good*.

I have something better for you.

When I wake, the words that aren't my own fall out of my mouth, filling the dark silent room. **I have something better for you.**

It was more a vision than a dream. I know that may sound funny—actually, I know it does—but I can't deny the truth that it brought to my life.

I have something better for you. I considered the words an actual promise from God. I didn't know what that something was, but I believed it might be better and bigger than my current crushed hopes. When I was baptized as a child, I heard His calling on my life, and this was a renewal of that.

This something was something bigger than me, yet still intimate. It was personal.

The promise didn't magically repair my faith, but it definitely helped. It didn't suddenly make my doubts disappear; it didn't take away my feelings for Jack right away. Somehow, it was more important than both those things.

The more I thought about it, the more I felt a sense of freedom. I was given an opportunity to trust something I didn't quite understand.

I have something better for you. Later I would have trouble really believing this.

"Is *this* what you had in mind, God?" I'd ask a few years later. "Is *this* better? Because it doesn't seem like it."

5

I never wanted the jam until Nick had it in his mouth.

He stood at the kitchen counter, scooping spoon size portions of sweet strawberry jam out of its jar, eyes locked with mine and a smirk on his face.

"Ple-ease?" I whined.

"Mmmm." He closed his eyes as he took another bite. "Yummy." The store-bought jam was an unnatural bright red. There were no actual strawberries in that jar—just sugar and food coloring.

Nick was three years older than I, a competent man in the sixth grade. Our moms were best friends, so his family stayed with us whenever they were in California. Usually, he only paid attention to Abby during a visit, who told him that I was "too little." But that didn't stop me from following him around.

"Can I please have a bite?" I could already taste the syrup-like glue coating my tongue. I didn't even like jam. But he made it look so good, so enticing. If Nick liked it that much, it had to be good.

"Okay." He held out the spoon in the air towards me, welcoming me to a shared experience.

As I leaned in to taste, he snatched the spoon away and back into his mouth. He laughed, his cheeks full of the sticky sweetness I so desperately wanted. I lunged at him and he darted to the side and out of the kitchen. I followed behind him, screaming his name over and over. "Nick! Nick! Nick!"

He ran down the hall, heading towards my room.

"Nick! Nick! Nick!"

Just as I caught up to him, the door slammed in my face.

"Let me in, Nick!" After jimmying the handle, I pounded on the door with my fists.

"Go away, Anna," he said. "I won't give you any."

"But it's my room. You have to let me in."

He didn't respond. I pictured him sitting by my bed, maybe kissing one of my stuffed animals with his sticky lips.

"Please?" Another pathetic whine.

No answer.

I lowered my fists. "Please?

≈

Though Nick remained in my life, I forgot about the jam incident of my childhood. Things that once feel urgent tend to fade with time.

Later, after my senior year of college, other things taunted me: church boys, the mirror.

And now, death. The change in seasons usually made me a bit melancholy, but the new changes in my life that came with the end of high school exaggerated the darker mood. I couldn't stop thinking about death, about my own mortality.

My feet dangled above the pond water, red toenails skimming the surface of the pond. It was hot, and I could feel the beginnings of a sunburn on my nose and cheeks —I'd probably have some new freckles. The evening heat, unusually humid, still radiated off the dock, and I knew I wouldn't be able to sit there much longer.

I'd gone to the neighborhood pond that July afternoon for isolation, stayed because it gave me a private sense of importance.

I liked the melodrama of it all, me sitting on the dock in a green sundress, hair down, contemplating suicide for the first time. I felt romantic, like Catherine in *Wuthering Heights*. I'd become acquainted with her at the end of the school year.

I also felt sad and lonely. Friends were scattering to different colleges, and, while I wanted the independence, I also didn't want to leave home. It was a fear of leaving. But there was also the heavy mood that had settled on my chest the past few weeks, a sort of sadness that I couldn't explain. I'd felt depression before, but it was surprising how familiar it was. Why did my depression come and go as it did? Down. Back to normal. Down. Maybe I should've questioned it.

C'mon. Do it. The voice that had taunted me during my freshman year was back again.

I thought about jumping in the pond and holding my breath for as long as I could. I would force myself to sink. I didn't want to die, at least I didn't think I wanted to die, but thoughts like these wouldn't leave me alone.

You have to do this.

When I imagined my body bloated and puffy being dragged onto the grass, I scooted away from the edge and closed my eyes. No. No, I didn't want to do it.

∾

A week later, I was away from the pond, breathing in mountain air.

My dad asked me if I wanted any water, and I said yes. I wasn't thirsty, but it was an excuse to catch my breath. We went hiking up at a family ranch in Breckenridge almost every other week that summer before my first year of college, but my lungs never adapted to the mountain air.

The meadows were especially green this time of year. The grass was happy in the sunshine, the creeks full. I liked all the pink elephant flowers and wild daisies and would probably pick a few before heading home. But there were also the hills covered with dead pine trees, ravished by a beetle species over the past ten years. Most of the pines were dead or dying.

"You tired?" Dad asked.

"No, I'm fine." I knew that we had to go at least two hours in order for Dad to get hungry. Post-hiking hungry Dad equaled giant pieces of pizza from Giampietros, our favorite.

We continued up the trail, keeping an eye out for moose and deer and talking about the upcoming weeks. I was depressed, and he knew it, so his questions were carefully crafted, unobtrusive. Any time I mentioned depression, my dad took to watching me closely, as if waiting for something else to happen. What was the something else?

"Nick's going to be here for a couple of weeks," he said. We had reached the north side of the ranch and stood to admire the view.

"Nick?" Something flipped in my stomach.

"Yeah, there's a special counselor he's here to see. He's going through a hard time."

I thought about the last time I saw him. Our families visited each other often. Had he been in college? Or was it high school? Whenever that was, I remembered his girlfriend walking into his family's kitchen on one of my own family's many visits. She was annoying because she was beautiful, skinny, with long dark hair. I'd slinked into the office, away from them. I didn't want to look at her.

I wanted my relationship with Nick to be that of hidden passion, like in the movies—maybe he secretly knew my potential and one day would reveal his attraction to me. He'd ditch the dark-haired girl for me, his brown-haired true love. In reality, my relationship with Nick was nothing more than a big brother, little sister thing. My feelings were intermittent with time. I'd forget about him and then, when he was around again, I was smitten. I felt like a rubber ball, bouncing up or down whenever I saw him.

"I can hang out with him. Abby will be out of town," I told Dad.

Whenever his family visited, Nick usually spent his time with Abby, as they were closer in age. They'd been close for years, and their friendship grew during their time at the same college. They ran together in the mornings and had meals regularly. I didn't know what made me more jealous—that my sister got the time with Nick, or the other way around.

Dad paused before saying, "He's here for special counseling, Anna. He's been going through a hard time, and his parents wanted him to try something new."

"Yeah, I know. But he won't be doing it all day, will he? We can be buds." I was the rubber ball again, this time back up.

Another pause. "You need to be careful."

"What? Why?" This was interesting. I'd never heard my dad say that before.

"He's in a bad way... and you're a pretty girl. I just want you to be careful."

Looking back, I wish my dad had never said that. I know he meant well. But because it was out of character —he never said anything really authoritative—it was all the more intriguing. It made me want to be anything *but* careful.

~

Nick arrived in the evening a few days later. I sat on top of the granite countertop and listened to my parents talk with him at the kitchen table. They were giving him one of the cars for his stay so that he could come and go. I waited for him to look at me.

I liked the way his dark hair curled at the edge of his ears. I liked the way he tended to smile whenever he talked. His voice wasn't exactly deep but it was rich, creamy almost. From where I stood, I could smell him, his cologne a pungent spice sprayed too liberally that morning.

When his cell rang, he apologized and answered. Apologizing again, he said it was his girlfriend and stepped out on the patio to talk.

So, he had a girlfriend again. Big deal. I mumbled goodnight to my parents and left for bed.

I went upstairs the next morning and, after rummaging around for some cereal, found him outside on the kitchen patio with a cigarette. I balanced my Cheerios with one hand. "Excited for college?" He exhaled smoke a little too close to my face, leaning back onto the stucco wall.

I shrugged. For the entirety of my senior year, I'd been exuding confidence for the next year, hoping college would suit me better than high school. I crowded my closet with college regalia, posters and sweatshirts, and submitted applications two months before the early deadline. But now? August loomed like an unknowable presence. High school ended, and so did my routine. I liked having plans. I liked being in control. But at this stage in my life, I felt like I didn't have control of anything—not of the future, and especially not of my depression.

"It's not that big of a deal. College, I mean." He'd just dropped out, with only half a year to go. "Want a cigarette?"

"I'm good." I was an American child of the 90's and a teen of the 2000's; I was told smoking was only for old men with rotten teeth and people with a death wish.

Nick was born on the cuff of the same decade, so what did that mean?

"Look, I have this counseling thing all morning, but we should hang out after," he said.

"Maybe." I couldn't be too excited. But I was excited. He wanted to be with me.

Over the next few days, Nick and I did things together —talked mostly. Went on walks. He had a way of asking questions that were too personal, probing when I was reluctant to answer. He was very interested in what I had to say: "Really?" or, "That's fascinating. Tell me more." And I did tell him more. My mundane eighteen-year-old life came spilling out, details tumbling out without much thought other than *he wants to know.*

On one of our neighborhood walks, I told him about Jack, about rejection. I told him about Abby and her fiancé. Randy was the only guy Abby had ever dated. They'd met her first year of college, and, despite friends' complaints that she was too young, she decided that her search was over, so the wedding plans were set in motion her senior year and were to culminate just before I left for school.

Surprisingly, I wasn't jealous. How could I be, when I saw the looks she and Randy exchanged? When I watched a grin pulling at her lips or cheeks reddening as she read a text message? She was *happy*, and not even I could begrudge her that. Randy was the ideal guy for Abby, and everyone knew it. My whole family adored him.

On more than one occasion, Nick's cell phone would interrupt our conversation, and he'd leave abruptly, his dark voice melting into a honeyed, *Hey, baby.* It annoyed me that he'd just leave like that, and it annoyed me more that it was the girlfriend. I knew he wasn't talking to her like he was talking to me—I hoped—so why did he talk to her at all? He never went all the way out of earshot, and I listened unabashedly. I knew that he knew I was listening, which made his purring all the more maddening.

Of his life, he spoke with a sort of hushed reverence, shrouding details that made him more mysterious.

"My life is an open tomb," he'd say.

"I don't want to know the purpose anymore," he said, another time.

He was proud that he didn't believe in God anymore and liked shocking me with his momentous discovery. I wasn't really shocked, though, even if he thought otherwise. I wasn't as afraid of doubt as I once was—God and I had made it through so far.

His conversation was thick with profanity to prove his allegiance to a newfound atheism, as if "fuck" could really be a middle finger to our conservative Christian upbringings. This *did* shock me. He'd contemplated suicide too many times to count—he spoke as if he were proud of it.

In all of it he used elaborate metaphors, both startling and puzzling me with what he was really feeling. "God is a vacuum—there's nothing but questions and empty space," and the melodramatic, "My soul is raining today," whatever that meant. I felt like I was playing a game of *Clue*. There was Colonel Mustard, in the study with Nick, killing God. Then there was Miss

Scarlett, forcing him to sleep for days in a depressed stupor.

It was his depression that he talked of most, more so when he discovered mine. I imagined that it was what he was supposed to be talking about with his counselor, but it seemed he was saving it all for me. It made me feel special.

~

We were standing outside the car in the movie theater parking lot with a few minutes before the show. I leaned against the front, feeling the lingering heat of the car against my legs.

"You've tried, haven't you?"

"Sort of." It wasn't true exactly, but I'd thought about it. Did that count? I wanted to tell him. I wanted to bond. Maybe if he cared, I was worth something.

"How?"

I told him I didn't want to talk about it. I did, but it felt strange since he'd actually attempted before. It felt like an odd thing to have in common. Besides, I'd only thought about it. I didn't actually want to do it.

"Just tell me." His voice dropped like it did when he was on the phone.

"Drowning. But I didn't, you know, try or anything."

Something flashed on his face and then disappeared. Disappointment? I felt like I was letting him down, but I was afraid to keep talking about it. I wanted the bond, but talking about suicide made it feel like a viable option.

He started to ramble about the greatness of oblivion,

something he'd done before, until I reminded him that I liked watching movie trailers and wanted to go in. We went into the already dark and rather empty theater, and he picked the back corner of the highest row.

I sat straight, so aware of his closeness that I thought I felt the hair on his arms touching mine. He whispered to me throughout the movie, something that usually irritated me. I wondered if this was what a date felt like, this hyper-awareness. Not that he was dating me—he had a girlfriend, remember?

For a few minutes, I pretended I were she, sitting next to the guy I probably kissed all the time. I was the girlfriend, with thin tanned legs and inspirational wrist tattoos, the way I imagined.

In the movie, *Midnight in Paris,* a man goes back in time to meet great writers like F. Scott Fitzgerald and artists like Picasso. It was a cute movie, one I'd see again. In one scene, the protagonist is in the car with Ernest Hemingway talking about his many lovers. Hemingway asks, "Have you ever made love to a really *great* woman?"

Nick whispered in my ear, touching my knee briefly as he leaned over. "Have you ever made love to a really *great* woman?"

I smiled back at him, uncomfortable with the repetition. Sex wasn't something I talked about with my girlfriends, let alone a boy. (Maybe just because I'd never had the opportunity.) But Nick was older than me, more experienced, and I figured if he could talk about sex, so could I. I wasn't in high school anymore; I was grown up now, and I wanted him to know it.

I repeated the movie line back to him. Quickly, as if I hadn't thought twice about it.

In the car on the way home, Nick pushed one of his Adele CDs into the player. He'd introduced her to me earlier that day.

"God, she's so sexy," he said.

"Definitely sexy. That voice."

"Anna," he paused. "You're pretty, too."

Just pretty? Not sexy?

I looked out the window. "Are you going to call your girlfriend, or what?"

He thanked me for reminding him.

～

We decided to go on a hike a couple days later. We left after his counseling session, so by the time we got to the trail the day's heat had set in. The back of my black T-shirt was quickly damp, as was the bridge of my nose beneath my sunglasses.

As we chatted, I realized I wasn't so much physically attracted to him as I was attracted to what was coming out of his mouth. Very much unlike me, he didn't care what he looked like, and I liked it. Maybe I could be so interesting that I didn't care what my body looked like. Probably not.

For the first hour, he talked about the girlfriend. I kept nodding my head even though he was in front of me and couldn't see it. I felt like his personal sponge, soaking up everything he felt for her. I could feel the jealousy rising, the jealousy that had already been there, and it tasted sour in my mouth. She's beautiful. She's smart. She's *sexy*.

"She's really insecure about her body. I'd break up with her, but she needs me for reassurance."

I need reassurance, I thought. Was I beautiful?

You are redeemed.

I need more reassurance, God.

"She needs me—I validate her."

"That seems like an awful amount of power," I said, surprising myself.

"I like power. I like making girls fall in love with me."

I wondered if he knew I was one of those girls. He wouldn't be telling me if he did, right?

A few minutes later, we circled back, avoiding a small snake that had planted itself in our path. We found a bench on an overlook where sagebrush scattered the ground and giant rust-colored rocks jutted out of the hill. We sat side by side, staring ahead.

"So, can I ask you a question, Anna?" He stretched his arm out against the top of the bench. His fingers grazed my shoulder.

I liked it when he said my name. "Sure."

"Do you ever think about just letting it all go? Abandoning all your inhibitions? Throwing out everything you think is right and just... I don't know, going for it? Letting go of fear?"

This was a typical Nick thing to say, so naturally I had no idea what he meant.

"Going for it?" I asked.

"If you're not afraid, you stop caring about how you're supposed to act. You stop caring about being safe.

What if we just let go, without abandon, right here, right now?"

I froze. Cracked my knuckles. What did he mean? I felt silly in my silence, as if I were a little girl again, not mature enough to understand. I suddenly felt aware of how alone we were.

"Have you ever made love to a really *great* woman?"

I didn't say anything. I got up, tried cracking my knuckles again—the tension wouldn't crack—and told him we should be heading back.

When we got to the car, he pulled out a cigarette and leaned against the car like we'd done the other night.

"Why do you smoke?" I asked.

"Because I don't care about my life anymore."

"That's kind of a stupid reason."

"Yeah, well. I'm *depressed*. Want one?" He held out the pack.

He wasn't just offering me a cigarette. He was inviting me to the darker thoughts I'd been pushing away. Was I beautiful? Was I?

I thought about the drowning. I didn't care about my life either.

"Yeah, sure."

~

That night we sat on the back patio. He'd just finished talking to her, so when he made a joke, I didn't laugh at it.

"What's eating you?" he asked.

"Nothing. I'm fine."

"You're mad."

I told him I wasn't, realizing I probably was. He should've been with me—not her. He'd already told me she wasn't "wife material." He'd told me everything wrong with her and, later, everything that was right with me.

"You're so kind. You're such a good listener."

This meant I was wife material, didn't it? He made me feel good, like I was worth something. Maybe he secretly liked me, was just baiting me. Was that a good thing or a bad thing? I didn't know.

"Tell me what you're thinking."

I like you, that's what. I couldn't tell him that. Not when I knew he didn't like me back.

"What do you want me to say?"

"Just tell me what you're thinking."

That I like you? I knew if I said it, I'd regret it. I'd never said that to anyone before. Why was he asking me when he was with someone else? It was like he could read my mind, but just wanted it said out loud. *I like making girls fall in love with me.*

I wanted to just say it, get it out there. But I couldn't. Why? Why couldn't I just do it?

I was eighteen, never loved—not like that—and the thought of outright rejection was too intimidating.

"You know what?" he said, interrupting my train of thought. "You should come to Chicago next week. I'll be there for this weekend concert thing. You should come."

I quickly told him I'd come. He didn't know I liked him, so it was somehow okay. He wouldn't invite me if he knew my true feelings. He wouldn't lead me on—I really wanted to believe that. Maybe he didn't know how I felt after all.

His phone rang. He stood and answered, smiled at me, and stepped away. "Hey, honey."

I went inside and downstairs to my room. I sat at my desk and started to look for flights to Chicago on my computer. I'd just buy the tickets and tell my parents afterwards. They'd be glad I was finally doing something again and not just sulking by myself.

~

I was entering my credit card information when I heard the sliding door open in the living area outside my room. Nick was still on his cell, but now on speakerphone. His voice was low but loud. I leaned back in my desk chair and listened.

"Yeah, it's ridiculous. They have so much money," he said.

I went to my door but stopped. I wanted to hear what he was saying about my family, but I felt the dread immediately. I stepped behind the door.

"Rich people," the girlfriend sighed. "They are, like, so full of themselves."

"Right?" He was standing just on the other side of my door.

She laughed.

It was weird, hearing him like that. I didn't know he felt that way about us.

"So, I was with Anna earlier and—"

"Anna? The one who's like, in love with you?"

"Yeah—"

"You told me she wasn't there."

He sighed and told her that I was there after all. That he wasn't with me all that much.

"She's just a puppy, following me around."

"You're a liar," she said. "You've been hanging out with her, haven't you? Why are you hiding it from me?"

"No, I promise. It's nothing. She's no one. She's nothing. I promise." He went back outside.

$\sim$

N o one. *Nothing.* I shut the door quietly, clicked out of the airline browser window, and went to lie down in my walk-in closet. My breaths were muffled face-down in the carpet.

I know it's dramatic, the way the suicidal thoughts came flooding in. I was a naïve little girl with my feelings hurt, I realize that now. It wasn't his fault. The tipping point is never the true culprit.

I lay there for a few minutes before going into the bathroom and turning the handle in the bathtub. I didn't like myself. And he didn't either. I stared at the water and wondered how hard it would be to stop holding my breath.

You are nothing.

But what would God think?

Be strong and courageous. Never will I leave you.

The voices contradicted each other, as they always did. I turned the water off and went back to my closet. My reaction to what Nick had said suddenly seemed too drastic, too foolish, even to me. I lay there for an hour and then two.

～

I avoided Nick until he left. I made up excuses—a headache, a book I wanted to finish—to get out of spending any more time with him. He bought it all (at least, I think he did) and didn't seem to mind my absence.

Abby got home from her fiancé's the night before Nick left. She was tired and grumpy from her travel and went right to bed, only talking to Nick about Randy for a few minutes before she did.

I went into her room around midnight and climbed clumsily into her bed in the dark. We'd parted several weeks before on an argument, I don't remember what about, but I had the urge to hide someone safe. I don't know why I felt Abby was safe. But I did, and it felt right.

She woke up to my crying.

When she rolled over and asked me what was wrong, I sobbed it out, the details getting messy and tangled together.

"I'm nothing, Abby. Nothing. He knew I liked him all along. I'm nothing." *I like making girls fall in love with me.* I was such an idiot.

"Am I not beautiful? Why couldn't God make me beautiful?" I cried. "I don't know if I can be courageous, like God says."

She rubbed my back gently, maybe touched that I came to her, and said over and over that I *was* worth something, that God loved me. Abby's kindness that night stayed with me. Despite all our differences, I knew she'd be willing to hold me when I needed it.

I sobbed some more and sucked in air like I was choking on my own snot. I didn't cry again for two years. That one night exhausted me: of my tears, sure, but also of my dignity.

~

When I confessed to my mom about the suicidal thinking, she pushed for more information about the self-harm. I couldn't talk to my dad, not after he'd told me to stay away from Nick in the first place. I think my mom thought my story was juvenile—she said I was the one who read into things, after all—but she took my drowning thoughts seriously.

"How do you feel about seeing a psychiatrist before you leave for school?"

"For what?"

"I don't want you thinking about this stuff anymore. I think you need some help. You know your dad has bipolar—we need to take precautions."

Precautions? I was depressed, not bipolar. Why would she even suggest that? That was inconceivable—I didn't even understand what bipolar was.

I was diagnosed with depression and started on a low-dose anti-depressant just a few days later. I didn't like the psychiatrist very much because he was abrupt and seemed a little nonchalant about something I thought was very serious. It scared me a little to be taking drugs that affected my mind. But in three and a half weeks, the heaviness lifted and I felt excited about my freshman year of college. I didn't care if my brain chemistry was being altered, as long as I felt better.

～

Nick turned into a bitter memory. He was forever enmeshed with my thoughts of killing myself. Have a cigarette; your life doesn't matter.

I couldn't forgive him because I couldn't forgive myself for wanting him so badly. Half a year later we met up for a brief talk. It was his idea, to "catch up." I don't know why he wanted to—we weren't really friends.

I thought that seeing him again would help me put it all behind me, so I agreed. I got to the café early, ordered and paid for my latte ahead of time so that it in no way resembled a date. He was fifteen minutes late.

"I want to talk about last summer," I said as soon as he sat down.

"Well, thanks. Hi to you too."

"It's just that. Well. I think we should talk about it."

"Okay. Shoot." He was acting too friendly.

I relayed the events back to him, trying to explain the way he affected me. The long talks, the girlfriend, overhearing his conversation. My thoughts came out rapidly, proof that I'd been thinking about what I was going to say in advance. I tried to control the waver in my voice, but I knew the emotion was coming through.

He was quiet when I finished. I hated how calm he was, the way a grin pulled at the corner of his mouth.

Then, "I'm sorry, Anna. But I just don't remember any of that. I really don't believe I did anything to lead you on.

"*Really?*"

"I think you were reading into things."

"But that phone conversation."

"I don't remember that. Sorry." He thought I was making it up.

"Look." He drummed his fingers quickly on the table, not looking at me. "You were young. It's understandable." He acted embarrassed, not of his past behavior, but of mine. He looked up and gave me what looked like more of a wince than a smile. "It's okay. You don't have to feel bad."

We both went quiet for a minute. I felt my heart beating faster. I needed to defend myself. I bit my lip, hard, before speaking.

"I don't feel bad. But you should."

He tilted his head, eyeing me as if he was trying to understand what I'd just said. I'd never spoken to him like that before, so directly.

"So, how's your family?"

Changing the subject, just like that?

"They're fine." I stood up and grabbed my purse. "You know what? I'm done talking to you." I didn't know what else to say. I wanted to point out the gaslighting, but wasn't sure how.

I left the café with a sense of injustice; I was angry at how he dared to make me feel foolish, angry because I knew I was right, but proud of my courage to leave.

6

I decided that I wanted to be a Democrat during my freshman year of college. It sounded cooler... and I liked the idea of "rebelling" from my family of origin. I decided I wanted to be a lot of things that year. (Things I didn't understand and things I would probably recant later.)

It was a year of changes, as can be expected of any eighteen year old leaving home for the first time, and the political decision was just one of many. I joined the hipster movement with my nose ring and five-dollar giant ugly sweaters from the local thrift store. I decided I *actually* liked coffee—and liked it black and five times a day. I found that environmental science was more interesting than my Bible class and psychology more interesting than philosophy. I started using a bit of profanity here and there—though nothing *too* profane. My language deteriorated—I even began to speak in hashtags. (#Literally.)

My Christian college was different from all the other

religious institutions I'd grown up in: there were more countries represented in my class than there were U.S. states. We all worshiped the same God, but diversity was encouraged. Democrats could be Christians too? Catholics weren't going to hell? Gay people were good people? Imagine that. It was like I was wearing a new set of glasses.

I liked the fall colors that popped up around our small campus—reds, yellows, oranges. The trees were so much more vibrant than they were in Colorado. I gathered some of the fallen leaves and hung them above my window with some twine. Soon snow would come and with it the frigid Illinois cold that would cut through clothing and go straight into the chest. Denver had snow, of course, but it also had sunshine. I'd have to get used to the permanence of gray sky.

Crushes developed and disappeared quickly. There was Matthew, my first date and a disappointment. I'd been waiting my whole life to be asked out, and even though the 6'8" basketball player looked promising, the date was a dud. We sat in the Rainforest Café, trying to hear one another over the loud monkey and bird noises squawking from the speakers above our heads. Mist sprayed my back from the plastic tree behind me. My gaze went from my salmon, to Matthew, to the little children running in-between the tables, and back to the salmon. Out of all the restaurants in downtown Chicago, Matthew had chosen somewhere worse than Disneyland. The two of us had nothing in common and nothing to really talk about. It ended in an awkward hug and a relieved goodbye. The date I'd been waiting to have my entire life? Easily, and sadly, dispensed with. It wasn't satisfying, and I didn't bother to wonder why.

There was Corey, the guy next to me in my statistics class. I played dumb, pretending like I couldn't understand the material so that he'd offer to help me after class. (Okay, so I wasn't totally playing dumb. I really didn't understand stats.) He did help me, and I'm pretty sure he caught me staring at the cluster of freckles on the side of his neck. When he lost his textbook, I let him borrow mine, but not before writing a fake to-do list and "leaving" it as a bookmark. I hoped the list would make him think of me. Number six on the list: "Find date for Friday night." (It didn't work.) The other problem with my plan? I didn't end up learning the material. My professor suggested I drop the class before I failed.

I started to feel the pressure to volunteer somewhere during second quarter. Volunteering seemed to be a given. There were so many super-Christians around, volunteering at hospitals and afterschool programs and nursing homes, intimidating me with their holiness. I wasn't doing anything but homework and watching *Downton Abbey* with friends, so I pressured myself into finding some sort of ministry.

I found Chicago's Beloved by accident. A boy who sat next to me in chapel mentioned "some guy" who started a homeless ministry downtown and told me to talk to "another guy." "Another guy" gave me the email address of "the guy" who, when he got my email, told me to meet him at the train station Saturday afternoon. It felt like a drug deal.

I didn't know what a homeless ministry entailed. I'd

never even met someone who was homeless. I'd grown up on a golf course and a polo field. But it sounded nice, like the "right" thing to do.

And besides, I felt like God had blessed me more than I deserved. I had a loving family, good friends, and a school that I adored. My depression was gone and, in its place, was a buzzing sort of energy. I *owed* something to society, didn't I? I needed to give back.

~

Hunter and Jake met me at the train station, their arms full of grocery sacks stuffed with bagged lunches. I was surprised at how old they were—out of college? Hunter was an attractive blonde, which made me glad I had chosen to wear my green sweater. It matched my eyes, so it was arguably my best look.

"We meet everyone else—you know, the other volunteers— at the Ogilvie Station," Jake said.

"So, we just hand out food and stuff?"

The guys looked at me.

"Uh, it's not really about the food. Food just starts conversation. We're going for the conversations. They can get food pretty easily already." Hunter sounded annoyed. "All they want is food—that's what *everyone* thinks. As if not having money means you aren't complex."

"Oh, right. Yeah." So, what were we doing? I thought food was the point.

The train ride was a quick forty-five minutes into downtown Chicago. The guys didn't really talk to me, but I was content to listen to them talk to each other. They were seniors at DePaul, but Hunter lived in the suburbs near my own college. They spent the ride complaining about some guy in the ministry who was "too enthusiastic."

"He's new. I guess it makes sense." Jake's eyes flicked over to mine.

We met everyone else, about ten other people all older than me, in the station.

"Basically, we break up into groups of two or three. Walk around. Talk to people, pray with them if they want it. Then meet up in a couple hours for dinner. Sometimes we treat people," Hunter told me.

"So, what do I say?"

"What do you mean?"

"I mean, when I talk to people. How do I know what to say?"

Hunter, again, looked irritated. "Just say what you'd say to anyone else."

"Right." I felt like an idiot. I wanted Hunter to like me. But I still didn't understand.

"You're not their savior, okay? Don't try to be a savior." He saw my embarrassed look, and his voice softened. "Just be a friend to people. You're not going to solve any problems."

I didn't know what he meant.

"Look, just come with me. You'll see."

~

Participating in Chicago's Beloved (CB) completely changed the way I thought of ministry. It wasn't a neat, pretty evangelical organization with rules and proper procedures. It was more like hanging out with people I'd normally not even talk to. I started joining Hunter and Jake on the train every Saturday, getting back sometime after 9:00 p.m., in time to crawl into my bunk, exhausted.

All of my preconceived notions were broken. Growing up, I had picked up that if you were homeless, it was your fault.

"He's just lazy."

"She has two hands. She can get work if she wants to."

"They're on drugs. If you give money, you're just supporting their bad habit."

Those were the things I'd heard in school growing up, so, before CB, I hadn't thought twice about passing by someone holding a cardboard sign. Now that I'd actually taken the time to talk with people who were homeless, I couldn't hold those assumptions anymore. They were just excuses that kept me from listening to my conscience. Excuses that kept me from giving a shit.

CB introduced me to a system that was broken. There was such a thing as a "disadvantage." Racial inequality. Wage gap. Complexity. Things I'd never even heard of before.

Every person on the street had a story. I guess that's common sense—of course everyone is different—but I was coming from the social class where we put poor people in a box and left them there without even realizing it.

There was Jamal, a guy who sat outside Giordano's.

"I'm sick of pizza," he said. "People try to be nice and give me pizza. I eat a lot of pizza. But what I really need is some help with my rent."

There was Isaiah, who didn't have family like mine to make sure he was getting to psychiatrist appointments and taking his medication. Isaiah talked to imaginary friends and liked catching bats with his sweatshirt. Every time he saw me, he gave a giant toothy grin and a bear hug that made me feel like I couldn't breathe.

There was Natalie, the woman whose story changed from week to week, depending on how much money she needed. Sometimes she had an ulcer, sometimes she didn't. Sometimes her mom abandoned her, sometimes it was her dad. Sometimes she was pregnant, sometimes she wasn't.

There was Joel, who had no interest in rehab, and there was Chris, who did. There wasn't a mold that everyone fit into.

Hunter taught me that there was a fine line between compassion and naivety. A fine line between compassion and arrogance.

"If you're going to ask if you can pray for them, you need to ask if they can pray for *you*. It's not like you're better than them."

"For God's sake, don't stand over her like that when you talk, Anna. How would you like if someone did that to you? Sit next to her. But, first, ask for her permission. Don't assume."

"You don't want to be like all the other Christians out there, do you? They're so arrogant. So stupid sometimes. They ruin it for the rest of us."

There was an edge to Hunter, an impatience that only seemed to grow over the weeks I knew him. He was exceedingly self-righteous about not being self-righteous. But he seemed to develop a soft spot for me, feeding my desire to impress him.

◦

I believed—and still do—that Christians are called to love others, and I started to realize that I needed to actually practice what I believed. "Do unto others as you would have them do unto you." That's what I'd said before, to my friends and to myself, but what did that actually look like as I grew into adulthood? Scripture taught that I was to live unselfishly, not in order to win any kind of favor from God, but simply out of gratitude for what God had already done for me. I grew up observing my parent's generosity with their money and with their home—we often had people living with us—but it wasn't enough to live in their shadow. I needed to have my own version of giving. I didn't have much money of my own, but I could give my time.

◦

"Hey, Hunter," I answered the phone, pinning it between my ear and my shoulder as I pulled on pajama pants.

"Wanna go downtown tonight?" he asked.

I shimmied out of my pajama pants and reached for my jeans. "Sure."

"We can stay the night at Jake's, do the art museum in the morning. Then CB."

"Yeah, sounds good."

My roommate, Leigha, looked on dubiously as I took my time packing a small duffle. We were friends from high school and now best friends.

"So, you're staying the night with them?"

"Yeah..."

"You. Staying the night. With *boys?*"

I shrugged. I wanted to feel grown up; I wanted Hunter to like me. I didn't want to act sheepish about something that was probably totally normal. This didn't have to be a big deal.

It felt like a big deal when Hunter and I walked into Jake's apartment after our late dinner. I suddenly became hyperaware of myself, awkward, and quiet. There were six guys standing around the small kitchen, all drunk or on their way there. Not really my scene.

I stood against the wall, ignored, and studied the wood laminate flooring. Laminate, the imposter, pretending to be the real thing. I hoped I looked cool and relaxed, like, "Sure, I do this all the time" but I'd never been around a bunch of drunk guys all by myself and didn't like the way it made me feel. I'd never felt so small. I'd never felt more like a girl.

Around midnight, after just standing there holding a beer that I wasn't drinking, I told Hunter I was tired and wanted to sleep. He took me to one of the back rooms.

"It's quieter back here," he said.

"So, where should I, you know, sleep?"

"You can sleep in Kyle's bed." He pointed to the unmade one in the corner.

"Kyle?"

"He works late. Be back in a couple of hours."

"So... okay." I didn't want to share a bed with a man I didn't know—heck, I didn't want to share a bed with a man I *did* know—but I didn't want Hunter to know that either. It would make me seem, what was the word? Inexperienced?

"He may not even come back tonight. But you're fine. He doesn't like girls."

He waited for me to understand.

"Anna, that means he's gay."

"Oh. Well, I guess it's fine then." I still didn't want to share a bed with a man I didn't know, gay or not.

"I'll tell him to sleep on the floor."

~

Hunter and I did the art museum the next morning. The big man-slumber-party hadn't been too bad after all, but I was still relieved to be out of the apartment and around other people. I was starting to feel a little uncomfortable around Hunter, so I walked ahead of him in the museum, breezing by any plaques on the walls.

We had a few hours to kill before we met up with

everyone else at Ogilvie, so we spent the time talking over cheap coffee in a donut shop.

Hunter explained how he and Jake started the ministry a few years before, when they were fresh out of high school, and how disillusionment quickly set in.

"You just learn not to buy into it after a while."

"Helping people, you mean?"

"Are we *really* helping?" He took a vicious bite out of his donut. "Are we making any difference? No."

"I think homeless people want someone to talk to, like anybody else. That's what you told me. You said that friendship is the only real thing we're offering. And friendship, to me, seems worth it. We're not doing this to make sweeping changes. We're just a group of kids. You said that too."

"Yeah, I said that, didn't I?"

I got up to refill my coffee and to have a minute to myself. I couldn't figure Hunter out. Some Saturdays, he seemed full of religious zeal and raging at "the system." Other times, he just seemed angry with himself.

"I think God wants us to do the best that we can do. That's it. We just try to love people like we would want to be loved." I sat back down and handed him a napkin for the sprinkle stuck to the corner of his mouth.

"Like God exists. No. Seen too much."

"If you don't believe in God, why are you still doing this?"

"I don't know, honestly. Helping people but making no *real* difference whatsoever? It just pisses me off."

I didn't know what to tell him. He was the experienced one, not me. What did I know? Would I become like Hunter, the more I did homeless ministry? He seemed so jaded.

"Helping the homeless is an expression of gratitude. That's why I do it."

"Bullshit. It's a way to feel better about yourself."

"Do *you* feel better about yourself?"

"Nah. I feel worse. I'll never be able to do enough."

"So, what? You just stop altogether?"

Hunter sighed. "Probably."

Was I doing this just to feel self-righteous? Hunter made me question my motives. Every Saturday, I felt like I was doing something right, something good, though I had to admit it was wearying. I *was* getting tired out; those Saturdays were exhausting, especially emotionally. For now, at least, God was calling me to this.

Feed my sheep.

I felt His quiet push—that familiar murmur—every time I second-guessed it.

≈

Tim started coming to CB in December, right around the time Hunter stopped showing up after he said he was "just done." I missed seeing Hunter, but I also felt more at ease now that he was gone. So, I think, did the whole group. It was like the perpetual thundercloud had finally cleared, giving us a little more of the open sky.

Tim was a big man: close to around 6'7" with the girth of an offensive lineman. He wore an enormous bushy red beard and a gold double lip ring. His too-tight collegiate sweatshirts did not go with his combat boots, and the hole in his jeans revealed a large tattoo of a Native American in sunglasses on his upper thigh. It was hillbilly meets punk rocker meets pseudo-hipster.

The two of us hit it off the first time we were paired together for a route. It was an especially cold day, and there weren't a lot of people on the streets, so we spent the two hours talking as we walked, ducking in and out of coffee shops for a little bit of warmth. We had absolutely nothing in common, but I was struck by the gentleness he carried, so unlike Hunter. He was gentle with me, gentle with the people on the street, just by the tone of his voice and the way he carried himself.

I learned that Tim had dropped out of school a few years before—he was twenty-six—and was currently working as a manager in a brewery. He said his education —he read a *lot*—was self-taught.

"College wasn't for me," he said. "Plus it gives me more time for my house church."

"House church?"

"Yeah, like, we hold a casual service in my living room. I'm not big on corporate worship. I don't think it's how it's meant to be. Church is about community, living life together. You can't get to know somebody in a sanctuary."

I thought about my own church, the lines of chairs. My least favorite part of the service was the mandatory shaking of hands.

"Plus," he said, "You can't really drink beer in a church. You *can* in someone's living room."

We saw someone huddled in a sleeping bag as we

approached the cross street. I let Tim do the talking and watched him give the guy some cash.

The guy didn't feel like talking much, so we let him be and headed for yet another Starbucks. Despite my gloves, I could barely move my fingers and needed to thaw them for at least a few minutes.

"You gave him a twenty?" I remember Hunter always saying five dollars, tops, if any.

"Yeah. I was just going to use it on alcohol, so why shouldn't he?"

"That sounds like C.S. Lewis."

"I know. I like to plagiarize."

Later that night, Tim walked me back to my train. He didn't want me to be alone since it was so dark. The chivalry was funny coming from a guy in combat boots, but I liked it. He gave me a hug and pulled a pipe out of his pocket as he turned to leave.

Of course he smoked a pipe.

On my train ride home, I leaned against the window and closed my eyes. I wanted to be like Tim. I wanted my church experience to feel authentic, like his evidently did. There was just something about him, maybe the way he talked about God, that did seem real.

~

For the next few weeks, Tim and I did a route together. He started texting me during the week, so it felt like we had a friendship apart from Saturdays. It was the unnecessary kind of texting, the kind that showed he liked me at least a little. I let him initiate every conversation since I wasn't sure of my own feelings.

I couldn't decide if I liked him or not. He made me feel safe, which, now that I was in college, I was a little ashamed of. Was it sexist, to want to feel protected by a guy? I never thought about sexism when I was younger. Now I heard about it all the time, though I wasn't sure what it meant. There were so many feminists at school who made me feel guilty for even *wanting* a guy, let alone wanting to feel protected. Was it wrong for me to want to feel safe? With Hunter, I'd felt on edge, the opposite of how I felt with Tim.

But Tim and I were just so *different.* He had no interest in finishing school. Plus, he was seven years older, making his lack of ambition more off-putting than maybe it should have been. He was happy with his life the way it was; it was simple. He was happy with himself the way he was; I was never satisfied with myself.

Tim's optimism for the work we were doing never wavered, and he eased into a position of leadership naturally. He didn't seem concerned with doing ministry the "right" way, the politically correct way, but his humility made it happen anyway.

～

Tim wanted to visit a new homeless ministry he'd heard about, and I agreed to go with him. It was a church on the north side that held free dinners for the homeless on Fridays.

"I just want to see how they go about it," Tim said, "to see if we can learn anything."

We arrived late and snuck in through the back. There were red plastic tables set up throughout the gymnasium. Middle-aged people in white aprons were bringing out paper plates full of lasagna to the twenty or so men and women sitting down.

I sat, not totally sure of what to do. I was tired and cold and didn't feel like talking to anybody, despite my agreement to come.

"Here you go, sweetie." A woman handed me a plate.

"Oh no—I'm not... Well, thanks."

The woman pulled out the chair across from me and sat.

"Do you know Jesus?" she asked.

Oh gosh. I looked down at my stained hoodie and jeans. Did I really look...?

"He loves you, you know."

"Yeah. *I know.*" I was surprised by how aggravated I was.

"Let me pray for you." She started praying. It was a long prayer, and the more she said, the more infuriated I felt. The lady didn't even know me. I hated her inane prayer, and I hated her assumption.

When she was done, she leaned over and patted my shoulder before leaving to find another victim. "Life will get better, honey. Just hold on."

Tim walked over from where he'd been sitting a few tables away.

"That woman totally thought you were homeless."

"Now I know how it feels. She was so patronizing." I glared at the woman's back.

"It's funny, if you think about it. Reaffirms what you know *not* to do."

"This is exactly the type of person that Hunter hated. That I hate."

"Anna, have some compassion."

"*What*?" Was he seriously taking her side?

"At least she's trying, right? Most people don't even do that."

"She just shoved Jesus down my throat without even asking first."

"So it was the wrong approach."

I shook my head. I didn't want to see her point of view. She thought I was poor and assumed I didn't know God because of it. So presumptuous.

"Calm down. Maybe we should leave." Tim put his hand on my shoulder.

I shook his hand off. "Let's go."

~

After that experience, I started wanting to prove that I wasn't like other Christians. I understood the poverty gap, didn't I? I had compassion. I wasn't starry-eyed with a savior complex, and I was proud of that. I didn't push Jesus on people—just offered.

When I overheard someone mumble, "Beggars can't be choosers," as he walked by someone with a cardboard sign on the street, I wanted to run after him, scream about his entitlement. When I saw a girl drop a half-eaten sandwich in someone's lap, avoiding any eye contact, I apologized on her behalf. I congratulated myself on my friendships with people on the street, on my ability to connect in ways that others didn't even try. *I* was the real Christian.

I didn't realize that I was the one being judgmental. My ministry turned into a sort of arrogance. The piety was contrived, a way to feel better about my rich upbringing. In another way, my "compassion" made me angry with everyone else. I was especially frustrated with other Christians, who just didn't seem to handle ministry the right way. I started to scoff at the woman handing out Bibles—didn't she know how that looked?—and the new girl at CB who thought people never lied during their hustling. *How naïve.* I had no compassion.

I skipped a few Saturdays, and then a few more. Every time I went to CB, I grew increasingly annoyed with others, which only made me annoyed with myself. Why couldn't I be like Tim, whose softness never turned to stone? He never grew tired with the Saturday routine, and it was frustrating me more and more. My annoyance seemed to quiet God's nudging that I go.

"I think I'm bitter. Bitter at everyone who doesn't *get it*," I told Tim. He was walking me back to catch my train. It'd been a long day. Lots of people out. "I don't want to be bitter."

"Maybe you should take a break for a while."

"I'll feel guilty."

"That means you definitely need to take a break." He looked at me. "But I'll miss you."

~

I stopped going to CB pretty abruptly. I told myself I'd go back, but I never did. Told myself that there was no point. Was I really making a difference? Now I knew how Hunter had felt. I probably felt the exact same way.

Tim and I continued to text, but whatever was there on his part—or could've been on mine—fizzled out because we no longer saw one another. But I felt his absence more deeply than I thought I would.

Tim was more like Jesus than I could ever be. He was gentle; he was kind. He was a little bit of a weirdo, but he was a safe weirdo; it was part of his charm. His compassion seemed genuine—nothing corporate, as he said. And, unlike me, he was patient with people, even the ones giving Christians a bad name, the ones who could've known better. I wish I could've been more like him.

~

I think God may have stopped telling me to participate in CB, not because it wasn't a good thing to do, but because it wouldn't have been genuine. Serving God with the wrong motives or a bad attitude kind of defeats the purpose, doesn't it? Or maybe that's a cop-out. Maybe I stopped listening to Him when it came down to it. I don't know.

Now, whenever I see a homeless person on a street corner, I try to make eye contact and smile, and sometimes I send a little prayer their way, but that's the extent of it. I superciliously pride myself on not making assumptions, on seeing them as *people*. Still, I give in to the inconvenience of not talking to him or her—wouldn't it be presumptuous?—and tell myself that next time will be different. But it never is. I've become very adept at not listening to God's prodding when I don't want to. It's a learned skill.

God's voice is a tricky thing, I think. Sometimes I hear it so clearly and have no doubt of what I'm supposed to do. Sometimes, it's more like a hesitant whisper, and I wonder if it's just a thought of my own. Sometimes I don't hear it at all, and I have to interpret the silence the best I can. And, of course, there are times when it's replaced by the voice that is much more sinister. It's a voice of Satan himself, the voice parading as a chemical imbalance. Back in the CB days, that voice purred in the background, biding its time: *I'm coming for you.*

7

I'd waited for the "something better," over the entirety of my first year of college, but nothing really happened. How could I *not* be expectant? My freshman year went well: I learned a few things here, met a few friends there, and that was it. What grand thing did God have in store for me now?

Excitement. That's what I needed. I was an independent woman. Alone and free to do whatever I wanted. Why would someone like me go back to live at home for the entire summer? Live with my parents again? That was the *old* me, not the *new and improved adult me*. I was nineteen now. Working at the GAP down the street from my parents' house for the summer wasn't enticing. (Neither was babysitting.) So, when the chance for travel arose, I took it. Adults travel, so that's what I wanted to do.

Given an opportunity at school, I decided to spend my summer working at a hostel in Amsterdam. It was a Christian hostel, and the staff—all volunteers—were encouraged to engage travelers in discussion about the Christian faith. It could be fun to be in Europe for a summer and, hey, since my parents weren't too fond of me backpacking around by myself, working at a Christian hostel was the best compromise.

I was assigned to go to with two other girls—Katie and Chelsea. Before our training started in Amsterdam, we went to Belgium for a week, where we were supposed to start practicing evangelism. We stayed in a variety of hostels, and I quickly learned that there is a reason that we should've taken the online reviews more seriously before making a booking. When a hostel only gets one star... it really only deserves one star. One of the hostels—the one that smelled like urine and weed—had naked plastic mannequins adhered to its walls and pink stuffed bunnies in every corner, like something out of a horror movie. As we walked up the creaky steps to our dorm, a woman passed us and whispered, under her breath, that we should not use the sheets. Bed bugs. Chelsea, Katie, and I were too afraid to be alone in the coed bathroom, so we all squeezed into one grimy, tiny stall when we showered that night. Actually, it was a good way to start a friendship, as we had to get over our awkwardness quickly. Fortunately, the other hostels were cleaner.

I wanted to learn how to *really* evangelize. I'd done a lot of it during my time in CB, but we typically didn't share the gospel with people on the streets—we shared stories, but that was it. Now was my time to learn. I know it may sound strange, this "evangelizing." It typically brings to mind a crazy person standing on a street corner with "Jesus loves you" and "You're going to hell" posters, or an even crazier person preaching Scripture through a megaphone at passersby. That wasn't the kind of evangelism that we were taught in the training sessions months prior. Instead, we were to practice "conversational evangelism" and "friendship evangelism." Instead of preaching at someone, I simply shared about what God had done in *my* life, and let the conversation go on from there: I'll tell you my story, and you tell me yours. If a person wanted to talk, we talked, and if they didn't, we didn't push it. The last thing I wanted to do was to preach fire and brimstone. That's not what Christianity is about.

Chelsea, Katie, and I made friends in Belgium easily. Hostels are conducive to meeting people. Travelers are open to talking about different ideas, eager to share their own thoughts and listen to new ones. Many travelers are out to "find themselves," which ultimately means they're open to learning about different worldviews. This made it easy for me to bring God into conversations. One night, we read Scripture with the guys in a room next to ours, just because they wanted to, and we talked late into the night about the concept of redemption. The next day, we wandered around Antwerp with a girl from Australia who wanted to share her own Buddhist beliefs.

Talking about these kinds of things made my faith seem more exciting, more real. I prayed on my own a lot more, talking to God throughout the day like He was another traveling companion, and it felt like I had a friend urging me on.

Feed my sheep.

One morning, I wasn't feeling well, so Chelsea and Katie went to a museum, leaving me alone for a few hours. As I lay there, a phrase floated into my mind, interrupting all other thoughts.

Let go.

I knew immediately that this wasn't just my own thought, and I began to pray frantically. What did He mean? Let go?

"I'm going to let go," I told Katie and Chelsea when they returned.

"What are you talking about?"

"I'm going to let go of anything that is holding me back so that I can fully embrace this summer."

"Like what?"

"I don't know. I think I'm supposed to be uninhibited —fully open to whatever this summer brings. Something like that."

I knew that this summer was going to be different. It was going to be exciting, and I was going to let go of anything holding me back.

~

I arrived in Amsterdam starstruck, dragging my large duffle across the cobbled streets and over the canals, staring openmouthed at the locals riding bikes and texting at the same time. I tried not to show my obvious curiosity at where the Red Light District might be. It was tulip season, and colors spotted the gated gardens and window boxes. The sky, pregnant with rain, seemed to welcome me in its way. I especially liked the Jordaan area; I liked how cafés intermingled with the skinny, four-story homes. Amsterdam charmed me with its candid and relaxed quaintness.

I took to the program naturally. Within days of working there, I could easily direct people to the Anne Frank museum, just a few blocks away, or to Café Winkle, where there was the *best* apple pie that only the locals knew about. I worked the front desk and, between checking guests in and out, had plenty of time to talk to people lingering in the café. Why wasn't I my usual introvert self? I don't know. Something about Amsterdam slipped into my veins. I became vivacious and smiley, eager to meet as many people as I could from where I sat as a receptionist. Maybe it's because I knew I'd never see those people again. I could "put myself out there" with no long-lasting repercussions.

I'd never met so many different kinds of people. So many cultures crowded into that tiny hostel, and I felt like I got a taste of each of them—just by observing, mostly. I laughed and batted my eyelashes with the rowdy group of Italian men. I patted the shoulder of the young Spanish woman crying about her ex-husband. I hid from the older Welsh man who I knew was trying to ask me out. I went to the museums several times with different guests. I became friends with a Portuguese woman because she complimented my outfit; I became friends with two French sisters because I complimented theirs. There were so many people who so easily became friends.

When backpackers walked into our hostel, they were usually eager to talk to someone new. Either they'd been traveling alone and felt lonely, or they were sick of the friends they were traveling with. This made conversation easy, even if a translation dictionary was a necessity. Going out for pancakes and a coffee with a stranger wasn't that strange.

I especially loved living in the staff house, which was a few streets up from the hostel itself. It was a large home with several common rooms, a kitchen crawling with mice, nine bedrooms, and two bathrooms that reeked of mildew. There were about sixteen of us volunteers, all somewhere in our late teens to late twenties. I was just one of a few Americans, but everyone spoke English. Even though I was just there for the summer, most of the staff members were hired on for a year, which meant everyone knew everyone. Once a week, we held "family dinners" out on the terrace, and there would be a mix of ethnic food brought to the table. Polish sausage, *hagelslag* with toast, and sauerkraut. Chelsea and Katie would contribute the pizza.

We were all Christians, but there was something unique about experiencing Christianity from other cultures. The core principles were the same, but everyone spoke of God in a new, fresh way. We all worshiped the same God, but diversity was encouraged. We did group Bible studies together in the living room each day, and I liked how my friends interpreted passages to mean things that I'd never even considered before. I felt like my eyes had been peeled open, because God was no longer an American. He was multicultural.

Thank God that there were (almost) no attractive guys in the house. I'd decided to abstain from romance for a while, letting go of something that would potentially hold me back.

~

Then I met Javier.

I came back from my morning shift, tired but happy, after a lunch of *poffertjes*, small soft pancakes, and *kaas*, flavorful cheese, at the hostel, and walked right into a conversation in the staff commons. Several of my friends were sitting around the lumpy couches listening to a man I'd never seen before.

He was handsome. Dark all over: eyes, hair, and complexion. Beautiful Spanish accent.

I sat beside Katie and Chelsea on one of the couches and tried to follow the conversation. Javier was talking about how his parents met. An elaborate story of a chance meeting on a ship, the kind you read about, the kind that doesn't happen in real life. True love at first sight—that sort of thing.

"And then they found out she was pregnant, and well, then begins *my* story."

"Wow," Mary breathed. She was the only one I didn't like in the house—dramatic and too pretty.

I listened a little more before everyone got up to go make a late lunch, leaving Javier and me alone in the room.

"Already ate," I told him.

Javier looked at me, noticing me for the first time. "Who are you?"

"Anna."

"American?"

"Yeah. I'm new. Well, been here a couple weeks." Was it bad that I was American, or good?

"Javier. I worked here a year ago. Now I go to school here in Amsterdam. I come by sometimes."

"You're a good storyteller."

"Well, if you tell me about yourself, I might say the same of you." He reached out and touched my hand.

I blushed.

He invited me to come with him to the weekly street market, one of the go-to places for fresh vegetables. I debated with myself for nothing more than a millisecond and accepted his offer. I liked carrots, didn't I? There was just something about him—I had to be close to him.

We went, walking aimlessly through the winding, cobbled streets, looking into people's windows. So many kept their curtains and blinds tucked back, allowing any passerby to see straight through into the living quarters, to see what was sitting on the kitchen table or what book lay on an empty chair. I knew this openness came from the Protestant tradition, and it was as if they still wanted to prove to their neighbors that they had nothing to hide. More often than not, there was a large cat sitting on the windowsill, a witness to my prying eyes.

Finally, we found the street lined with booths of colorful produce.

Conversation was easy. I don't remember what we

talked about, but it turned personal quickly, as if planned. I kept straightening my blouse over and over. It wasn't cleavage I was going for, but maybe something close.

It began to rain lightly, but we walked without really noticing, away from the market and back through the narrow side streets and over canals. A few ducks floated down on the shimmering water, and a biker, one hand on a handle and the other holding an umbrella, passed by quickly without noticing.

"So really," I said, "I'm not all that interesting. Pretty boring, actually." I said that despite the fact I'd tried to talk up my life—hiking in Colorado and going to downtown Chicago every weekend. I *did* hike a lot when I was home. I *did* go downtown during the school year.

He laughed. "Yes, you are. And what do you study?"

"Not totally sure. Psychology probably. I don't really want to follow my sister's footsteps, if you know what I mean. Abby's a writer, and I want to pave my own way."

~

I'll always remember the afternoon I spent with Anne midsummer. She was from Norway, and we'd started chatting about our different homes after she checked into the hostel one evening. We decided to go the Van Gogh museum together the next day.

After wandering the floors for a few hours, we sat in the museum's café with too-expensive cappuccinos. We talked about Van Gogh's depression. It intrigued her just as it did me. I told her about my own struggles and about the medication I was on, and she told me about her own mild depression.

"God has been faithful through it all," I said.

"Are you a Christian?"

"Mmhmm. Do you have any beliefs?"

She shook her head. "I see religion as a mental coping mechanism for people who can't handle difficult situations by themselves." Her words sounded practiced, just as mine often were.

"Yeah, I can see how that would make sense. I *can't* handle difficult situations by myself. But I think I have something, someone, better than a coping mechanism."

"I'm afraid I'll only come to believe in God when I actually find that I need him," she said, "Everything is good for me right now, so I don't need a God. Which probably means something really bad has to happen to me first."

I nodded. I could see what she meant, even if I didn't completely agree.

As we walked back to the hostel, I thought about her words. I knew I needed God, unlike Anne. Though "something really bad" hadn't really happened to me. I'd been depressed, sure. But it wasn't like I was bipolar, like my dad. My belief would never waver—it *couldn't* possibly, now that I was older—but would my belief in God deepen? Did I need something really bad in order to know Him better?

~

I got a Facebook message from Javier a few days later. He said he "couldn't stop thinking about me." Wanted to "hang out."

Chelsea asked me why I seemed so happy, so smiley during my shift, and I shrugged her off. I was happy because—tada!—I wasn't pining. I wasn't pining after him, and *he was thinking about me.* Sans the pining. This was a first.

That afternoon in one of the empty rooms, I spent time with Javier and Cheeky, one of the other guys in the house and a friend of Javier's. Cheeky was from Argentina and played Spanish songs for us on his guitar. His voice was sexy and purring, and even though I had no idea what the lyrics were, it was nice to just sit there stretched out on the floor, listening. I felt Javier's eyes on me the whole time. Time was unimportant. We didn't notice the room darkening until Cheeky turned on a lamp in the corner of the room.

"So, movie tonight?" Javier looked at me. "There's an old theater that used to be an opera house."

"Sure," Cheeky said before I could answer. "I'll ask Katie to come."

Although the outside of the theater was rather ordinary, the interior was old and ornate, with rich, gilded wood carvings on all the door frames. We sat in plush but faded red velvet chairs and watched the screen lower in front of the stage. Ten minutes early.

Javier had pushed to the front of the line, and I'd watched him flirt with the pretty attendant to get free tickets. I don't know how he managed to ignore the annoyed looks of the disgruntled people still standing in the line behind him, but he did.

"He's quite the ladies' man," Cheeky said. "He gets what he wants."

Katie and I went into the bathroom before the movie started. She needed to pee, and I needed to check my makeup for the third time.

"So... Anna." She said through the stall. "I have a little dare for you."

"Oh, please no."

"I dare you to hold his hand." She knew I liked him. She also knew I was a virgin in absolutely every way—hand-holding was no exception.

"Don't think so."

"C'mon. Just hold it during a scary part of the movie. What do you have to lose? Be brave for a change."

What the heck, I decided. This was the summer of "letting go." I could give up my inhibitions for once and just embrace the experience.

The thriller wasn't at all thrilling, but I acted like I was nervous and reached for his hand towards the end. It was unbearably obvious. When I tried to pull away a few minutes later, he held onto my hand.

The movie over, we said goodbye to Javier and biked back to the staff house. Cheeky biked ahead, and Katie kept bumping into my back tire, trying to make me look back and see her winking emphatically.

"You like him." It was singsong. "He likes you."

She rode up next to me. "This is the first time this has happened for you, right?" She wasn't trying to embarrass me. She simply pitied my stories of failed attempts with high school boys. "Just go along with it. It's fun, isn't it?"

"Yeah. I think I *do* like him."

"He likes you. I bet you gave him a boner. Ha. Just by holding his hand. *Guys.*"

"What's that?"

"Oh gosh." She laughed. "You pitiful private school girl. I can't believe you've gone this far in life without some *proper* sex-ed. How old are you again?"

"Well, just tell me."

"How old are you—nineteen? Unheard of. But, hey, it's cute. Stay that way as long as you can."

"What is it?"

As we locked up our bikes, Katie explained to me the intricacies of the penis. It sounded horrifying; it sounded marvelous. I quietly cursed my inexperience.

∾

I was curious about sex. Going to private schools hadn't given me much information, just like Katie said, and I tended to avoid any discussions about sex when they did happen. I'd never had a boyfriend. And all *my* guy friends were private about that kind of stuff. It's not that all the Christians in my life were immune to desire—not at all. Since sex was supposed to be for marriage, I guess lust was simply kept quieter. Is that healthy or not? I don't really know.

After our conversation that night, I started asking Katie more questions. At first I was timid, but her nonchalance made me bolder. She encouraged me to be more comfortable with my body, to see the poetry of the Song of Solomon as just as spiritual as the rest of the Bible. *Your two breasts are like two fawns, twins of a gazelle, that graze among the lilies...* I hardly found gazelles erotic, but I got the general idea.

I'd been feeling more confident about my body in general, which is a little strange, considering I'd naturally gained some weight since starting college. I exercised and ate well, but my body wanted to change its shape despite my efforts. The old me wouldn't have been able to handle how my body changed, but I think I was too enmeshed in my ministries to really care. My mind simply didn't have room for any bad thoughts. When I was involved in service, my insecurities became insignificant.

~

Javier told me he'd be going home to Spain for the rest of summer and was leaving in just a couple weeks.

"So, basically, what I'm saying is that we need to spend time together before I leave," he said.

And we did. First, his dancing lessons one afternoon in the kitchen. I'd been cleaning up the remains of a staff lunch when he came in with an old CD player, the portable kind that I had when I was ten. This time, John Mayer. Not exactly dancing music, I knew, but when he took my hand, I just smiled. (And why, on earth, John Mayer, the known phony womanizer?)

I liked the way his hands felt on my waist, his breath on my neck. He smelled like rusty iron and spice, warm and inviting. I spun out of his arms and back into his chest, not caring that my dress swung up to reveal my upper thigh. This was Amsterdam, baby.

A few nights later we went to a concert starring a very bad singer and my very first beer. Staff members weren't technically supposed to drink, but I decided it didn't matter when Javier handed me a cold Heineken.

We stood against the wall of the bar, grinning at each other as the musician hit another wrong chord. I sipped my beer and smiled again, pleased with myself. This was me, all grown up, drinking, and flirting with a real live man. And he *was* a man. Four years older than I.

"You're so beautiful," he said. He'd leaned over closer to my ear so that I could hear him.

I blushed for the third time that night. "Thanks. You are too?"

He laughed. "You know something? We click. We hardly know each other but—you and me—we go together."

This time, it was my turn to laugh. His words reminded me of a cheesy pop song that I would've made fun of. Javier didn't have a problem with being cheesy, although it made me a little embarrassed. But we *did* click. This was my first time experiencing something mutual, and it felt pretty darn good.

If you'd told me months before that I—the doe-eyed, wanna-be-liberal, little evangelical—would be out late drinking with a man several years older than me, him stroking my knee and whispering in my ear, I wouldn't have believed you. It was too fantastical. Yet here it was, happening to me. *To me.*

What did he see in me? Maybe I was cute. Maybe I was fun to be around. Maybe I just needed someone to show me that.

Another time, we went hitchhiking to the beach on a rare warm day, catching two cars with our cardboard signs, just for the sake of doing it. It's something I never would've done without an attractive guy egging me on, and to this day I can't believe I did it.

The first car was difficult to wave down, but eventually an elderly woman stopped. She could only take us so far, but an Australian couple picked us up soon after that and took us all the way to the beach. They'd hitchhiked before, they said, and were happy to accommodate.

The day was warm, the sun out to warm our backs. We walked back and forth in the wet sand eating our *lekkerbekje*, crispy fish and chips, bumping into each other on purpose. He told me about his dreams of owning his own business, and I liked how he talked too quickly when he was excited. I told him that I dreamed of being a psychologist, even though it was a total lie. All I really wanted to do was be a stay-at-home mom, but I feared that would sound terribly disappointing. I needed to sound more ambitious, like he was. So, I made things up, consoling myself with the thought that they were things that *could* be true if I really wanted.

We caught the train back that same evening.

"I think you should visit me in Grenada." He was sitting on half of my seat, even though the train car wasn't full. He balanced himself by putting his hand on my thigh.

"Okay, I can try." I'd do whatever I had to do.

Javier liked to lie in the grass at the park and make up life stories of the passersby. It seemed like a romantic thing to do, of course, so I loved it. I'd lie on my stomach, and he'd lie with his head on the curve of my back. We were doing this one evening, narrating for a woman with a large dog, when it started to rain, soaking us within minutes.

"I know where to go!" He helped me up, pulling me to my feet.

We ran through the park and down a side street until we came to a small Arabic restaurant.

"I think it's closed," I said.

"They'll let us in."

The restaurant *was* closed, and I watched Javier haggle with the manager to get us a glass of wine. He gave us a table in the far-left corner and told us we had twenty minutes. I realized then that Javier really could get anything he wanted.

The table was close to the ground, and we sat on purple sequined cushions on the floor. The faux-crystal chandeliers were dim, and I studied the shadows dancing on Javier's face as he talked.

That's how it was with us: we talked and talked. About nothing, about everything. He pulled conversation out of me in a way that no one had ever done before. Maybe it's because he was so open himself.

In a way, he reminded me of Nick: so suave and sure of himself. But this time, even though we hadn't really acknowledged it yet, the attraction was mutual.

"Anna?"

"Yes?" I loved the way he said my name. The "a" sounded different, softer and more drawn out.

"I have a question for you."

"Okay."

"If I lived in America and we met, and if I asked you out, would you say yes?"

"Yes." Finally, out in the open.

"Hmm." He finished his glass. "Let's get going. Rain stopped."

I wanted him to say more on our walk back, but he didn't, and I didn't either. Perhaps we'd leave it like that.

~

On the Sunday before he left, we got lost on a bike ride. We were trying to find a church that was supposedly a straight shot forty-five minutes away, but I quickly learned that there was no such thing as a straight shot through Amsterdam's ever-curving streets. At the end of the forty-five minutes, we realized that we'd gone in a giant circle. And, as always and of course, it began to rain.

I'd chosen a dress for the day, despite the bike ride, only because it looked good on me. I wasn't embarrassed that the rain made it cling to my body; I was actually glad for it. Javier's looks made me feel proud of my body's curves, the ones I would've hated a year before.

We instead went to a church that was closer to the hostel. We were late and slid into some chairs in the back. The pastor was talking about "Freedom in Christ." I left the service feeling like I had "permission" from God to just enjoy what I had going with Javier. I didn't need to overanalyze. I could savor the experience for what it was. I doubt that that is what the pastor had in mind—in fact, I *know* that's not what "Freedom in Christ" is—but I took it for what I wanted it to mean. I doubted God begrudged me my fun.

We got back to the staff house before everyone else, and with the rainstorm raging outside, the inside of the house was quiet and dark. We startled a few mice as we walked into the kitchen. The rest of the house seemed like it was holding its breath. Javier made tea as I changed into a skirt and put my wet hair into a braid.

"The staff house needs a cat. All these mice." He brought two mugs over to the couch.

We shared a blanket and sipped our tea. I didn't know how to turn the air-conditioner off and told myself that that was the reason I leaned into him.

For a few moments, we didn't say very much. Who was going to bring it up? I mean, I knew he liked me, but we'd yet to talk about it. We sat in silence and listened to the thunder and water pelting at the windows, a haunting ambiance.

Finally, he confessed he liked me outright, and I did likewise. It was the moment I'd been waiting for all my life, the moment that should have slowed down, the moment I should be able to relay, and it was over in seconds.

But this was the first time this had happened to me: something mutual and verbally recognized.

We discussed the last few weeks, how we'd fallen for each other, and the upcoming ones when we'd be apart.

We would Skype, he said. Talk every day. I could visit him. See Grenada. I could learn Spanish and one day be able to talk to his parents. He could even visit me.

I had to leave for a shift, and we promised to talk later that night. It was like someone hit the pause button on my daydream.

~

J avier and I were back on the couch. It was a sagging kind, where two people sitting on either side eventually fall back into the middle. Cuddling was inevitable.

It was around midnight, and everyone else was asleep or just upstairs for the night. The light from the other room cast into ours, but otherwise it was dark.

Our conversation had dwindled over the hour, and I knew very well that he wanted to kiss me. It'd never happened before, but even I could recognize the taut awkward pauses for what they were. The air between us was like a knot begging to be loosened.

But this would be the first time, and I didn't know what to do. I was too aware of myself.

I was too old for this to be my first kiss. Who doesn't get kissed until nineteen? It was too embarrassing.

Our faces were close, and I kept looking away, uncertain. Did you use tongue on the first time? How was I supposed to know? Where is one supposed to learn these things if she hasn't stepped once into a public school? (Okay, yeah, people do kiss in private school. I was just oblivious.)

"Anna, you haven't kissed anyone before, have you?"

"Um. Not really."

"Do you want to? We don't have to."

"No, I do. It's just that I don't know how."

He smiled, told me he'd teach me, and then he did.

I always imagined that my first kiss would be short, relatively chaste. Maybe awkward, but bearable. Quick, but cute.

Instead, we made out for two hours. He was a good teacher. A great teacher.

"Anna." He and I were laying on our sides, facing each other, his arm around me to keep me from falling off the couch.

"Yeah?"

"Oh. Nothing." He stroked my cheek, then my hip.

"Anna?" His fingers ran across the top of my skirt.

I moved his hand to my shoulder and kissed him.

"Never mind," he whispered.

We spent an hour together the next morning before he left for the airport. On our way out the door, he pulled me off to the side and onto the stairs and kissed me against the railing. It was 10:00 a.m., and I felt woozy all over.

We went on a walk and ended at a park bench where he pulled me onto his lap. We kissed right there, in public, his hands roving. I couldn't help but be embarrassed by the few passersby, but he pulled me in close whenever he realized my eyes were wandering. I was much too conservative for this sort of thing.

"This is Europe," he said.

He continued to embarrass me—and thrill me—on

the way back. He kissed me against a wall, pinning my arms above my head. It was over the top, borrowed from movies, too much.

~

For the rest of the summer, we Skyped every day, even after I got home. I told my family that Amsterdam had been the best summer of my life, and they knew it had to do with Javier just as much as it had to do with the evangelizing.

But our conversations quickly lacked substance. The heat between us couldn't quite make it through the computer screen. We both knew it wasn't the same, giving it our best for a while anyway. The romantic rush was gone, the physical attraction buried somewhere in the memories.

Our exchanges got shorter and shorter, and, even though he planned to visit me at home before I left for school, he seemed to grow disinterested. He messaged me less and when we did talk, he asked fewer questions. Awkward pauses of silence—the wincing kind—worked their way into conversations. Was I no longer interesting? Now that he couldn't kiss me? Was he no longer interesting? Now that he seemed so far away? At first, it made me feel sad, but as the days went on, it mattered less. I didn't *really* know him all that well.

I wanted it to last, but clearly it wasn't going to end up like that. Even though I didn't want it to be, the romance was a summer fling—albeit a cool European one. Javier seemed more like an elaborate dream than a real person.

It was like I'd been holding water in my hands and watched it evaporate like steam.

We decided that he shouldn't visit after all. Things ended quickly. We didn't even have the stamina to do it over Skype: we texted it all.

"I don't know if I will make a good boyfriend."

"Then maybe you shouldn't come."

"Maybe you're right."

And that was it. At least it was mutual.

～

I found my mom on one of the lounge chairs outside by our pool. A big floppy hat shaded her eyes. August in Denver makes for very hot afternoons, unlike Amsterdam.

"You doing okay?" she asked. She'd been dealing with a moody daughter for days.

"I guess."

"You really liked him."

"It was fun for what it was. I have to remember that."

～

I'll always remember my time in Amsterdam with love. Doing evangelism strengthened my relationship with God, because I spent so much time talking about Him. I made good friends, and I carried their conversations back with me. I became more at ease with my body. And, of course, there was Javier.

I'd like to think that I learned something from him in

particular. I want to make sense of it, find some greater purpose.But I can't, not really. I don't think God was trying to teach me something. He gave me a gift, and I enjoyed it.

And man, what a hell of a first kiss. A fling in a foreign city? It'll be a good story for disbelieving grandchildren someday. They'll laugh at their doe-eyed, wanna-be-liberal, little evangelical grandmother.

8

"Y ou okay?"

Leigha caught me hiding for the first time in my dorm closet.

"Oh, yeah. You know, just feeling a little down." I crawled out, embarrassed, and rose to my feet, towering over my best friend's 4'11" frame. Even I could feel tall around Leigha.

"Well. Good. But maybe you should call your psychiatrist or something." Her smile was weak. I knew she'd text my mom if I didn't take her advice, which would feel more humiliating than it would intrusive. Leigha was my roommate, as well as my best friend. She worried about me.

Leigha, my protector. The roles in our friendship were silently acknowledged without a formal agreement. She watched over me like a sister, with weighted comments whenever I acted stupid. Or depressed. I was supposed to be the one to inspire, to encourage. "The Motivator," if you will. I wasn't really doing my part.

I couldn't even motivate myself. The fall of my sophomore year found me hiding in my closet on a regular basis. With homework finished in the mornings and meals eaten quickly—or not eaten at all—alone in the cafeteria, I could spend time in the darkness.

I'm a good liar and was even better back then. I could pretend that I was still outgoing and outrageous from the summer before, when I was in Amsterdam, the introverted and sheltered high school girl turned rogue. (Rogue for me, that is.) I faked a good smile.

But my depression, back once more, pulled me backwards and deep into the self I didn't want to be. What had triggered this? I was a bouncy ball, and my mood dropped out of nowhere.

Wasn't I better than this? I'd been through this before. "Feeling down" wasn't entirely foreign. It'd just been a while since that summer. With Nick.

Depression was a blanket draped over my head. I could breathe just fine, but I was somehow still suffocating. I could see through the thickly knitted fabric, but I couldn't move through my days quickly anymore. The feeling, this darkness, felt physical, like a paperweight pressing into my chest so hard that I wanted to cry.

I knew what freedom felt like. It felt like childhood. Like bicycling in Amsterdam just a few months before. Like kissing Javier on a park bench.

To appease Leigha, I called my shrink.

When Dr. Hart asked me how I'd been coping, I told him that my private prayers and devotionals saved me. God seemed like the only one I could talk to.

I thought I could hear him shrug through my cell phone. Forget faith—medicine alone did the saving.

"I'll prescribe you a higher dose."

Higher. Always higher.

Well, if it worked, it worked. That's what I figured. As long as it could be like the year before, the first year at school, full of expectant changes and the predictable growing up. I just wanted to feel better.

～

It takes a while for medication to kick in. It's an agonizing while, but there's a bit of hope attached, somewhat like a Post-it, a reminder in bold Sharpie, that feelings—brain chemistry—can change.

"You're going to get through it," Leigha always said. She started dragging me to dinners with her and our other friend, Alyssa. The two girls proved their loyalty by spending time with someone who wasn't very fun to hang out with. You know you have a true friend if she'll sit with you in the silence while you lie prostrate on the couch or staring at the ceiling. That's what they did.

I also talked to my parents.

Mom and I were close, of course, but it was Dad on the other side of the phone when I called. He knew about the "terrible sadness." He knew what it was like when it was too hard to get dressed and go to class.

Depression. We had that in common.

After I got back from Amsterdam, I stumbled across one of my mom's journals. I thought it was a kind of article, because it was a detached sheet of paper, not bound in any sort of notebook, with no "dear journal" at the top. I read hungrily, unaware of any needed privacy. Once I realized what I was reading, I couldn't tear my eyes away. In it, she wrote about their time together in China, where they served as teachers—this was before the carrot business and the seminary degrees. She wrote in detail about what happened during that time.

Abby and I were young when we lived there with my parents, and, though Abby has memories from our early life, I do not. (But since Abby remembers eating peanut butter and jelly sandwiches in a foreign city where local markets knew absolutely nothing of peanut butter, I tend to question the validity of her memories.)

I knew that the reason my parents moved back to the States was my dad's mysterious mania. I once heard my mom mention a "breakdown." In those eight pages of her journal and in our conversations afterwards, I learned more about the breakdown than I wanted.

It was a religious high turned manic episode. The impulses he interpreted as the Holy Spirit turned dangerous, spinning Dad's thoughts into a rambling and dangerous mess. He believed himself to be invincible, specially anointed by God. Dad saw chariots and horses of fire coming after him and bought a trombone because he'd always wanted one; he tried ridding my mom of demons. Then, Dad disappeared into the city, planning to run a marathon barefooted, and returned to bang on our door while my mom ushered Abby and me into the bathroom for an impromptu game of hide-and-seek from Daddy.

Mom had to send Abby and me to my grandparents'

California home for our protection. Would he kill us? Think he could fly off a building and take us with him?

She followed security officers as they rolled her husband up in the hotel floor's carpet and dragged him to a Hong Kong hospital. She watched as nurses tied him to a bed. From the security camera, she watched him pleading to be let free from the straitjacket, watched the steel door shut him alone in the thickly padded room.

Mom described the horror in detail and her own self-doubt—was this her life now? All they wanted was to serve God, to follow His will, and now this? In one week, she packed up our apartment, shipping her whole life back to the U.S. in boxes. Dad was transported to a hospital in LA, properly diagnosed, and thoroughly medicated. The entire trajectory of their lives changed overnight, forever.

My mom had no way to predict that, years later, he would be happy and flourishing in his new job as a chaplain and in our close-knit family life, medication free, faith strong but sane, the G-7 ward of the Hong Kong hospital a mere memory.

It was strange to think of that entire episode happening when I was just three years old. That man isn't the father I know now. I felt cheated out of something important. Did I notice my dad's absence? Did Abby?

I admired my mom for protecting us the way she did, and I respected her even more for staying with my dad. I don't think anyone would have judged her for leaving him. How could they? So many people leave their spouses nowadays, sometimes with the refrain that they weren't "the same person I married." For a while, my dad *wasn't* the same man she'd married. But she stayed, in sickness and in health. She managed to survive when her husband went insane. She chose to fight for what she loved.

My parents' marriage was strong. I wanted to find love like that, love that wouldn't leave me whenever things got hard.

Now, I wondered if she ever looked at him and saw that straitjacket. His occasional mild depression and anxiety were tiring, as they should be, to both of them, but it wasn't as frightening as what happened abroad. Was she afraid it would happen to Dad again? Was he? I tried not to think about it.

~

"Leigha, I think I'm going to be an English major." It was months after the closet incident, months into feeling better.

"Okay." She didn't look away from her computer. She was a procrastinator; a paper was due in an hour.

I liked psychology well enough. Becoming a psychologist: that was the plan. But I wanted to know Charlotte Brontë and Gwendolyn Brooks much more than I wanted to know Abraham Maslow and B.F. Skinner. The authors wouldn't help me make a living, but they were more attuned to what I wanted to be "my style." (I was still trying to figure out what I wanted that to mean.) Forget being practical.

I made the switch before going home for Christmas, filling out a slip of paper that meant a lot more to me than it did to the advisor whose signature was messily scrawled at the bottom.

I think the decision was important not only because it redirected my future, as all college studies do, but because I made the decision with a clear mind. Fog-free.

There wasn't a particular day or a particular moment when the depression left. It dissipated slowly, sending itself in wispy pieces, one by one, out the proverbial door. I noticed its absence only when asked about it for the first time, at home during break.

〜

"How have you been feeling?" Dr. Hart liked getting right to the point. He leaned forward in his chair, his elbow brushing the leaves of a wilting poinsettia on his desk.

Our sessions, even in person, lasted no longer than an *exact* five minutes. (I'm not exaggerating. One time, I timed it at four minutes.) He asked, I answered, and then I went to the pharmacy, resigned to feeling rather insignificant.

"Actually, a lot better. I think I'm on the up."

"Okay. Good. But I'll prescribe a higher dose—just so that you continue to feel this way." He scribbled something on a small square piece of light blue paper and threw his hand out in front of me. "Two hundred dollars today."

I left his office, looking down at the illegible words and numbers. I felt embarrassed by his jumbled scrawl, like it was hiding what was strange—wrong—about me. I could barely read the number of milligrams he was prescribing for my brain.

Higher. Always higher.

~

T he next semester, I took my pills with a swig of coffee every morning. Drinking it black, four to six times a day, and as much as I could get.

I signed up for as many English classes as I could. My 9:15 a.m. class starred Dr. Sexy Voice, a young professor whose purring southern drawl sounded like Matthew McConaughey.

I'd always been a good student. "If I'm not ahead, I'm behind." I lived by that. But by February, I strangely didn't care about my grades. They were unimportant; why had I cared so much before? They didn't have to mean anything about *me* anymore. I did the work, my best work, but I arrived late to almost every class. The attendance alone brought my perfect hard-fought A's to low B's —a first for me.

I couldn't seem to sleep at night. Eyes closed, mind buzzing. I stopped trying and spent hours on my computer instead. Lilly didn't mind the blue glow from my top bunk. I sometimes watched movies; mostly, I typed furiously and feverishly, writing lyrics to new songs. I'd never cared for songwriting before, never really understood it, but inspiration was mine. It felt both romantic and eclectic. Colorful creativity bubbled into vividness. I gave my lyrics to my younger sister by seven years, Elly, a natural musician who was especially talented for her age. She turned rhymes into chords on her guitar and notes on the piano. She congratulated me on my tangible and heartfelt emotion that came through the chorus.

And it was genius. Better than usual. I felt special—I was a true *individual*—someone with creative powers. The screen on the computer opened, and I flew through.

The nighttime writing made me tired during the day. My sporadic naps made me late, first by five minutes and then by twenty. I turned in my work, of course, and it won me the accolades I deserved, but soon my nocturnal habits walked into my classes. I listened to the lectures, sort of, as I filled pages and pages of my notebooks with songs.

"Anna, a minute?" Prof. Matthew McConaughey stopped me on my way out one morning.

I hoped he wasn't going to ask me about that day's class. I'd listened to his lecture but had heard absolutely nothing.

He fumbled with the stack of essays in his hand, rearranging them twice. "I'm just wondering if you're okay. You seem distracted, not engaged like you were. Your work seems, well, it's different." He smiled, but his eyes didn't.

I apologized. Told him I was having "sleep issues."

He nodded and frowned but didn't say anything.

I continued, "I'm not getting any sleep for some reason, so I feel, I don't know, distracted. I'll figure it out."

That's what I told another professor when she invited me into her office. I was a gifted student, she said, but said she was concerned about my work. My essays had a lot of careless errors. Good ideas, but too rushed.

Concerned? I didn't understand. Everyone else in the class could clearly see that I was the best, couldn't they? If only they could see more of my work—my mind was a *masterpiece*. Though no one appreciated my genius.

My new friends didn't help the situation. They probably made it worse.

~

"Ten burpees!" I didn't need to shout, but I liked that it made me feel like Jillian Michaels. Weeks had passed since my conversations with my professors.

My four new friends groaned from their mats on the floor.

"We've already done sixty push-ups."

"You're killing us."

I clapped my hands at my friends. "Let's go, people. You got this." I dropped to the rough carpet floor and into a push-up before propelling myself upwards in a jump. My arms ached, begging me to stop, but I could ignore it. Burpees were nothing. I imagined that other students were looking over at us, impressed with my ability.

I wondered if Peter was in the gym. He was one of the guys in my larger friend group, someone I noticed right away. I met him through the others and found myself sitting by him at our group's midnight dinners at Denny's. He was cute, and, though that was all I knew about him, I wanted to talk to him more. I craved the feelings that came with a crush—the rush of wondering if someone liked me. But anyway, there was the rest of the semester, and I had plenty of time.

I made the group do two more sets of ten before relenting, agreeing that the workout had been hard enough for today. We walked from the gym, inhaling the fresh air, and went back to my small room where I poured everyone a small cup of the chocolate milk from the jug I kept in the small black fridge by my bunk bed.

"You need your protein," I said. "Next time we'll do a dance workout." I downed the entire cup of milk, dribbling a little down my chin.

More groans.

"I can't believe you have energy for this, Anna. What time did you get to bed last night? We didn't get back from bowling until midnight, and you said you weren't tired."

"Last night? Three something. But I feel great." I dropped into another burpee just to prove it, danced a little in place, and then looked at the four of them, sprawled out on my bed, the futon, the floor. It was nice having more friends.

The group didn't mind when I started joining them at their hangouts and meals. I liked how spontaneous they all were, and I knew that I added to that spontaneity. You can get only so wild at a Christian school, but they made bowling nights into adventures and Star Wars movie nights into late-night marathons.

"So. Who's up for some something tonight?" I asked.

"Too much homework. Don't you have any?" One guy shook his head. "Never mind. I already know the answer."

Everyone knew that I somehow always managed to finish my work before any of the others. Okay, so I was rushing it like my professor had said several weeks ago, but I couldn't see how it suffered. I already filled every spare moment with homework or friends. I never had downtime, so why put extra work into the homework I was already doing?

"We could go out when you're done." I suggested. We went to get pancakes late at night all the time.

"I don't know where you get all this energy. It's crazy."

I shrugged. I didn't know where I got the energy either, given that I didn't really sleep anymore, but what did it matter? It just meant I had more time to get things done.

The slow and long days of the first semester, bogged down with my depression, transformed into busy go-go-go days. My new friends quickly knew me to be the funny one, the vivacious idealist. I led workouts. I led conversations. I led plans for spring break.

Where was this coming from? Was I even the same person from months before? Careful, thoughtful Anna. How could a person change so quickly? I didn't know. I didn't care. I was alive again, free.

My mind seemed so *loud*. My thoughts were constantly buzzing around, hopping from one corner of the brain to the other in random sequence. God's voice seemed to disappear in the meantime, and though I may've noticed, I oddly didn't question it. I surmised that I was simply too busy to care about serious things. And, for once, that didn't matter anymore.

❧

"I feel like I haven't seen you in forever," Leigha said when she walked into the room, setting her backpack by her desk chair.

I looked up from my notebook but kept tapping my pen against the page.

"You're my best friend, and I never see you anymore."

"Well, I'm here now." A few lyrics went through my head. *I'm here now.* Yeah, that was genius. I could turn that into a song.

Leigha sank onto the bed beside me. "At least you're not moping around anymore. Last semester was rough, wasn't it?" She pulled gently at a piece of my hair that was hanging on to the corner of my mouth.

"Mmmhmm."

"I was thinking you and I could do a spa day over spring break. Relax a little. We could use it after the midterms."

"Oh. I actually made other plans." I was a little embarrassed that I'd been spending so much time with the other friends—didn't want her to feel neglected—and hadn't told her about the spring break plans. She didn't fit in with my other friends, and I didn't want it to feel awkward.

"But you never pass on a spa day. Sure something's not wrong?"

"The gang is coming out to Colorado. Skiing and all that. My idea." I moved my hair over my opposite shoulder, away from her.

"You planned all that?" She knew I hated being the leader in a group.

"Yeah, it'll be fun."

"Just promise me you'll get some rest. You've been so busy, and I bet you're going to collapse if you're not careful."

"I feel *fine*." I didn't know why she cared. Her caution annoyed me—couldn't she get the hint? I was happy, wasn't I? So what if I was busy?

She noticed my tone, her head tilting to one side. "As long as you're feeling like yourself again, I guess it's fine." She squeezed my shoulder. "I'm just glad you're feeling better."

~

Spring break at my place in Colorado: my idea of the perfect vacation. Guys in the basement, girls in my room. Hiking, skiing, binge-watching TV shows.

I, however, was preoccupied with the text messages from Peter. I now knew he was interested in me. Hoped so, anyway.

Peter was quite built, the kind of guy who worked out his upper body in the gym once, if not twice, a day. Despite his size, he did not have a commanding presence. I liked that about him.

Peter was pleasant to be around; he was easygoing and liked doing whatever the crowd was doing. He was quiet; he didn't care about standing out. He was predictable; he ate the same three meals every day (protein, carbs, protein). We didn't have much in common, but so what? He loved God, I loved God—what was more important? I could pretend I, too, wanted to run a marathon and learn astronomy like he wanted. I could like his TV shows and movies. Yeah, I could pretend.

Peter asked me to my school's ball after the break, and we went with the entire group. I felt pretty in my long blue dress and crystal earrings and arrived at the venue at Navy Pier with a giant smile that was even more exaggerated by my lipstick. We danced into the night, and, when I walked outside for a quick breath of fresh air, I studied the water and wondered whether I might take a spontaneous swim.

I felt *free* lately, which meant time felt rushed and carefree.

～

After the ball, the number of Peter's text messages increased. Banter, mostly.

Thinking about u a lot missy

Me too

We should go on an adventure. Didn't you say you like adventures?

Let's go on the roof

Deal

Time hurried by. We started watching games together; we started going on walks, then, soon, out on dates. Late night talks replaced my frantic, *genius* songwriting.

I'm here now
I've been here all along
With my dear little honey
Just singing this song

We liked making out in the prayer chapel, which was in the attic of my dorm. My room was small, and Leigha was often there studying, so we had to be inventive. There was something about kissing on the thick blue carpet in a place of prayer that made it more exciting, like we were doing something naughty, even though we were just making out. A holy place became sacred in a different kind of way. We kissed for a while and then watched movies on my laptop—also not something encouraged in a prayer chapel.

"You're so outgoing. It's something I really like about you," Peter said. We were sitting against the wall, drawing pictures in the carpet with our fingers, and half-watching a movie.

"You're sweet," I said. "No one has ever called me outgoing before. My mom used to call me the careful introvert growing up."

"Really? That doesn't sound like you."

"I guess that's who I am now."

"Well, I'm glad for it. I really like you, you know." He leaned into me.

I smiled. "I know." I shut my laptop. "Movie's boring."

"We could read."

I shook my head. Peter read books like *Ten Steps to Success* and *How to Become Fit*. Boring books and nothing like the books I read for my English classes. There was no color to his books, no spirit. I wished he were a more interesting reader.

But I liked having a boyfriend. I was doing something right. Life was on track. I, this outgoing and happy *me*, was desirable. God wanted this for me—why else would everything be going so well? I was no longer the whiny teenager moaning about my lack of romance. I'd grown up. Life was good, and I wanted it to stay that way.

I had friends. Lots of them. I had my writing. I had *myself* back, the new and improved *me*. And now, with a boyfriend, I had achieved perfection.

I pointed to the small window above the stack of Bibles. "It's raining. We should go run around." I imagined I could smell the rain; it beckoned me.

"And get wet?"

"That's the idea."

He hesitated. "Why not?" He pulled me to my feet.

We went out for dinner on Tuesdays, made scavenger hunts for each other around campus, and, of course, kissed in the abandoned upstairs prayer chapel. I felt giddy; my butterflies were more like full-sized birds pounding from side to side. It was the romance I wanted, the kind of thing that was *supposed* to make my heart and thoughts race. I didn't know that they would've been racing anyway. Romance: the perfect cover.

It actually never occurred to me to question my newfound energy. It was fun, so why would I? That's what delusion looks like: the absolute inability to see what was right in front of me.

I scanned the room from where I sat against the edge of the couch. My professor's house was charming with its country French décor, but it was too small for the large group of students. She'd invited us all over so that we could "get to know one another." In other words: check each other out. I eyed some of them, trying to gauge whether or not we'd be friends during the upcoming summer study-abroad trip to England.

"How many credits are you taking?" April, the girl sitting next to me, asked.

"Ten. Trying to cram some English classes in." After our time in London, we'd be in Oxford for some extensive study.

"That many?"

"I'm a quick reader." I smiled at her. I had to pick a roommate, and she seemed cool, a two-second judgment call.

I watched some of the others, and then the tall guy who arrived late. I recognized him from one of my freshman psychology classes. Blonde, deep voice, noticeably tall. He was a guy I had been paired with multiple times in class; I think I'd attempted to flirt with him a few times before giving up. Rob something or other.

"Shit." Why did *he* have to be on the trip?

"What?" April asked. She'd heard me curse. A Christian who cursed? Now she thought I was cool too, a two-second judgment call.

"Oh, nothing. I know him, is all. He's nice."

I wondered if he'd remember me. Did I want him to? I thought about Peter. I had a boyfriend now, so it didn't matter if Rob remembered me or not. Rob was unimportant. But, just in case, I'd keep my distance. I wasn't supposed to like someone else, and I wasn't going to.

~

My study abroad trip started with two dull weeks on campus before we left for England. This meant eight long hours a day in the classroom with the same two professors. The rooms were unusually cold, and no number of layers could stop my shivering—though it kept me from falling asleep. I spent my time outside of class dutifully working on essays and stories in my room or exercising in the gym. Peter encouraged me to work out as much as possible. Maybe he noticed my weight gain, I don't know. I know I'd started to.

Peter began working at a youth camp at the start of the summer with little access to cell reception, so we were only able to Skype every now and then. The busyness kept me from missing him.

I was in love. (I thought.) This was going to be the perfect Christian romance: we'd date for two or three years and, probably, get married. His mom would make a good mother-in-law, after all. She was nice, and I liked her low-calorie, low-sugar, low-fat frosting.

It's natural that smaller groups would materialize out of a group of twenty-five, and, when we arrived in London, I and a few others made a pact of sorts to walk the city and museums together, to catch the tube and meals together. We looked quite the part, charging through crowds in order to keep up with April.

April, now my roommate for the summer, became the obvious leader. Her opinions were respected; every word was to be taken seriously. Even though she'd never been to England, she knew everything a tourist needed to know about how *not* to act like a tourist—a sin, indeed. I knew she thought my gym shorts and tennis shoes screamed *AMERICAN,* but she didn't say anything.

And then there was Rob. April walked ahead, bull-dozing through crowds with her phone GPS. Some others trailed in the far back. This left Rob and me in the middle, keeping the group intact.

I tried not to like him, so I knew I did. Couldn't help the physical attraction. Tall—I always *loved* tall—and a low bass voice? Hopeless. But physical attraction was easy to ignore. Couldn't I prevent my emotional interest? I tried not to bring up anything personal, sticking to our sightseeing. We talked a lot during our walks, keeping our conversations in the "friend zone."

But I was in trouble when we went exploring one evening.

~

"Who wants to go on an adventure?" Rob asked as he walked into April's and my room. Mary and Jason, curled up on my bed with a movie, begged off. April said she was tired and gave the couple an annoyed look. I said I would go.

The two of us set off with no real agenda, Rob's idea of an adventure. After a tube ride, we wandered around

Buckingham Palace and then ended outside the Houses of Parliament, right beneath Big Ben.

Rob and I leaned against the bridge, looking down at the water and across to the London Eye, the giant Ferris wheel going in slow, lazy circles. Black taxis whizzed behind us, and other tourists, out for the same reason as us, brushed by. The night's clouds covered any starlight, but the city's activity was light enough. We didn't talk for a few minutes, which felt surprisingly comfortable.

"Tell me more about yourself," I said finally.

I don't remember what Rob and I talked about first—books, probably—but eventually he started talking about his family. His grandfather had a small bison farm in Wisconsin; he'd grown up playing on the farm with his cousin, his best friend from childhood. His high school friends were like brothers; his actual siblings played Dı volleyball, and his parents watched every single game.

I could tell he was close to his family, just as I was to mine, and it got me talking, opening up about my own life. I told him about my parents, about my sisters and brother and about how we were different from one another. I even told him about the Javier fling, turning my last summer into a joke.

It was just a conversation, nothing more, but I went back to my room that night feeling intensely guilty, like I'd done something wrong.

I liked Rob's sincerity, his easy kindness, but, more importantly, I liked that he was interesting. Not quirky exactly, but something like it. He sat in the back of the bus, eyes closed and headphones in, and I liked to turn and look at him discreetly. Instead of music, he listened to poetry that his dad recited and recorded for him. He was obsessed with W.H. Auden—he was currently reading *The Age of Anxiety*—even more than he was obsessed with Shakespeare. (When we saw *Macbeth* at the Globe, Rob said the lines under his breath as the actors spoke.) There was something sweet about his adoring yet unpretentious love of literature.

Rob said he never went to the gym, and he wasn't embarrassed about it; he didn't care about "low-fat" and simply ate until he was full. He wasn't obsessed about bulking up his body. I noted this with interest. Everyone I knew, from my mom to those high school boys to Peter, was obsessed with his or her physique.

He was quiet but opinionated, speaking up only when asked. When he talked about God, his faith seemed unobtrusive and genuine—he always managed to relate whatever he was reading to his faith. I liked him, and I knew it. I had a boyfriend and was attracted to someone else? That wasn't supposed to happen.

That night, unable to sleep like usual, I wrote Peter a long email about how much I missed him in the dim light of the bedside lamp. *I think about you all the time.* And I did. When I wrote to Leigha, I talked only of Peter, avoiding any mention of Rob's name.

Life was perfect; I had a boyfriend. This was God's *something better* for me: no messing it up.

~

I didn't feel *quite right* during our last few days in London. I slept only in sporadic naps, usually in the middle of the day between outings. But I started having dreams that made me want to avoid going to sleep altogether. These weren't normal dreams. They weren't like God's *I have something better for you* dream. They were nightmares.

I am standing in a shower giving birth to a dead baby. The baby comes out in chunks as small, twisted pieces of tiny flesh. Then my throat starts to close, and I start to cough up small bird eggs, one after the other. The eggs begin to break in my throat, and I am coughing up bits of baby birds, all fuzz and moist pink skin, and then the eggshells. The edges of the white shells begin to cut through my throat, and I begin to bleed. I am coughing up bird pieces, shell, and long fleshy strings of my own throat. I am frantic, coughing just so that I can breathe. When my throat is finally clear, I look down at my feet, which are covered in blood, dead birds, and dead babies.

I did not wake up screaming, but in silent terror.

Then I began lucid dreaming during my naps. In a lucid dream, I was aware that I was asleep and could usually hear what was going on around me. I could control certain elements of the dream; I was the architect interacting with my subconscious. Whenever I realized that I was dreaming in real time, all I wanted was to get out, to wake up, to escape the hyperawareness. I could hear April moving about the room, but I couldn't move my body or force my eyes open. I was trapped within my own mind.

Eventually, I learned that I could wake up when I hurt

myself in my dream. I'd look for a piece of glass, building a dream room until I found one, and cut my arm until I could wake up. But over time, I had to become more drastic. I rammed myself into the walls I built, cut off limbs, and shattered mirrors with my hands—all to wake up.

I started to think about hurting myself even when I wasn't dreaming. I forced myself to look away from the tracks as trains approached in the tube station, but an image of my leaping body flashed in front of my eyes anyway. When April, who was naturally thin but worried about her weight anyway, made an offhand comment about my own weight, I envisioned myself stabbing my stomach, cutting all the fat away. They were violent images, and I couldn't stop them. I tried to explain the effects of my polycystic ovarian syndrome to April, but I knew it no longer seemed a valid excuse. I was still eating, wasn't I?

I called my mom the night before we left for Oxford. I was starting to wonder if something wasn't right with me.

"You have to help me. I don't know what's going on. It's so weird."

"Do you feel sad?" she asked.

"Not really. I'm having fun. But I have these thoughts." I didn't go into detail.

"I'll talk to Dr. Hart. He will know what to do."

She did and called me a few hours later; she told me Hart wanted me to up my anti-depressant—double it.

Well, he was the psychiatrist. I trusted him completely and gave up my concern. Higher, always higher.

~

"Coffee?"

I smiled at Rob. "Yes, please."

We took turns getting each other drinks at meals, a little ritual I started accidentally. Well, not accidentally, but it didn't have to be that big of a deal.

I'd often mentioned Peter—I always referred to him as *my boyfriend*—in conversations with my friends. Everyone needed to know that I was happy and that we liked each other a lot. I talked about Peter, so Rob was a friend, and nothing more.

"You not hungry?" Rob set a hot teacup down by my plate.

"Not really." I tried not to eat that much. Restricting my food was difficult, but it was the preferable alternative to feeling fat. I wanted Peter to see me beautiful, thin. There were no mirrors around except the one above the bathroom sink, so I was only able to imagine how ugly I must be.

I stood in my room, staring at the clothes in my suitcase. Nothing would look good. *Of course* nothing would look good.

You're hideous. Why that voice again?

I ran my hands over my breasts, stomach, and down to my thighs. Hideous.

I couldn't work out enough. I was hideous.

April had a way of commenting about what we ate— what *I* ate. I don't know why. She demonized the cafeteria's fried food and noted every time I bought yogurt and granola from the *Prêt a Manger* to replace it. She noticed when I started eating less and when I began pulling up my loose jeans. She congratulated me when I had to buy new, smaller shorts from a local store. I wanted the congratulations. I was doing something right, I thought.

~

I looked at the group of middle school girls in front of me, waiting for them to move. Like all the other tourists visiting Oxford for just a few hours, they were oblivious to anyone trying to move through a crowd quickly.

Finally, they noticed me and let me pass. I hurried by and squeezed through a group of boys speaking Portuguese. What tourists. I was one of them, of course, but whatever.

I walked for an hour before settling onto an obnoxiously orange-colored bench in one of the parks. I stared at the pigeons picking at some trash that was overflowing from one of the trashcans and nibbled on my ham sandwich, eating maybe a third of it.

Oxford kept me busy; I didn't have time to think about food. To get that many credits in such a short amount of time meant a lot of hard work. My work felt agitated, and I rushed through things to get ahead. Pumping out papers quickly: I needed to be faster, better. Even better than I'd been the semester prior. My urgency seemed more and more apparent, to everyone but me. I was completely deluded.

I thought of the day trip we'd taken a few days before to the lake district. My group had gone on a long hike through the hills, past the grazing sheep and along a creek. I'd felt *off*, but I couldn't explain what that felt like, so I didn't question it. For the most part, I ignored the racing thoughts and took artsy photographs. I took one picture from a short distance away, so that I could get my friends with the sunset in the background. Rob's tall dark frame stands out against the waning sunlight.

I tossed the rest of my sandwich next to the trashcan, easy access for the pigeons. What to do now? I was done with my essay and had an empty afternoon before our group tried punting, the traditional Oxford way of boating, along the river. Everyone else took way too much time on his or her schoolwork, and I tired of waiting. I stood up. I could use another walk. I couldn't sit still for very long.

In my spare time, I found myself wandering the streets during the day, speed walking with purpose to nowhere in particular. Oxford isn't a big place, and I became familiar with it quickly. When my friends were *finally* finished with their work for the day, we went to movies or to parks, pretending to fit in with the locals.

Later that day, we tried punting in the river. The water was more green than blue, and I dipped my fingers in and out, careful not to smash them when another boat bumped into ours. It was warm, and I could feel the heat bearing down my bare shoulders.

I sat in the back of the boat and let the others take turns steering the boat with the metal pole, caught up in my own chatting. I talked. And talked. I couldn't stop for the entirety of the boat ride, turned on by an invisible switch. The words kept spilling, joke after joke. Their laughing encouraged me, even when it turned into uncomfortable smirks. I couldn't stop.

Afterwards, April pulled me aside before dinner. I wondered if she was going to warn me about the fried fish sticks.

"What was *that*?" She placed both hands on my shoulders. I thought she was going to shake me. Slap me, even.

"What?" I stepped back.

"You're acting funny. Sometimes you need to know when to shut up."

Um, what? *Was* I acting weird? I didn't know what to say. I was happy. What was so wrong with that? April was a jerk.

~

I can honestly say that I had no idea of what was happening to me, not even in the beginning. I knew that my dad's bipolar disorder was genetic, but it *never* occurred to me that I would inherit it. How could it? My brain was broken—it wasn't working correctly. I thought that because I was already in touch with a psychiatrist, I was fine. A psychiatrist is supposed to handle the medication—Hart was the one who would notice a manic episode, not me. And since he knew my father's mental health history but never mentioned bipolar, it didn't seem relevant. Hart could only help me so much through the phone. And, really, could he have even helped me in person, when he charged me two hundred dollars to only meet with me for five minutes at a time? I trusted his judgment completely, and that was my downfall.

In a manic episode, you are completely out of touch with reality. You cannot see how differently you are acting and thinking. You are completely blind to mania until someone addresses it, helps you see it.

The mania in my mind kept me from seeing what should've been so obvious. I was sick, and I needed help. If I'd been home, my parents would've seen it immediately, but I wasn't. It would just keep building until it became dangerous. Higher, always higher.

~

Our return flight was canceled, and a few of us were stuck in a hotel near Heathrow for a night. Rob and I decided to make the best of it. We holed up in the hotel bar, reveling in the beer now that our chaperones were gone.

I didn't drink that much, so I think it was the late night that made me so open about Peter. I confessed that I was having doubts.

"I love him, but I don't really love him, you know?" I didn't feel like writing to him. I didn't feel like talking to him. Something was off, right? This wasn't how I was supposed to feel.

Rob gave tentative advice. I watched him carefully, hoping for something to flash across his face, but he seemed unaffected by my words. No matter how much I wanted it, he wasn't going to like me like that, so I couldn't let him influence my feelings for Peter. Still, I thought too much about our hug goodbye—had it been too long? Had I been the one to initiate it, or had he?

I fell asleep during my eight-hour flight home, slipping into another lucid dream. But I couldn't wake up—I couldn't wake up. How could I wake up—please, God, let me wake up—

I woke up. I'd shot myself in the head with the gun I imagined to be in my hands, in my dream world. Only when I killed myself could I escape my dreams. But the dreams didn't bother me as they should have. I was *too happy* to understand that I was going to kill myself.

9

I n three days, I am supposed to leave for school, and
I'm sitting in the garage and listening to the hum of
the car's engine and the voice in my head. It's time.
I am trying to kill myself.

Do it. You worthless piece of shit.

**Come, Thou fount of every blessing. Tune my heart
to sing Thy grace.**

Oh no you don't, no hymns allowed.

**Teach me some melodious sonnet, sung by flaming
tongues above.**

I am not sad—so why am I doing this? I don't make
sense anymore.

Tears streak their way down my face, the slow rolling
kind that pick up momentum at the cheekbone. I text
Dad, "When are you getting home?" because I'm afraid
he will come home before it is over. I don't want him to
stop me, and I do want him to stop me. I want to kill
myself, and I don't want to kill myself.

I look back at my phone. No response. Instead, Abby

wants to know what time we are meeting for lunch tomorrow. I wonder if I should lie and tell her noon. I won't be there.

Die. Escape. Escape from what?

I Google "how long does it take to die from carbon monoxide" and visit a few websites on my phone, and then I start to scream. The garage is large, but it won't take long.

My heart is pounding—I can hear it like it's coming from the radio. I can't stop the energy that runs down the veins in my arms. I can *feel* the energy like a drumbeat. It feels like panic, like fear, like excitement. It's too much. I'm too high.

"Help me," I scream into the steering wheel. I want someone to find me. Help me.

Bind my wandering heart to Thee.

Bind it, godammit.

Come Thou fount of every blessing.

Fuck you. Hey, that's a bad word. I never say that word. *I'll show you those fucking flaming tongues.*

Come Thou fount. Come Thou fount.

Dad texts back, "almost home, why?"

I don't want this, not with him seeing me. I turn off the engine and run up the stairs inside, not sure if I'm really dizzy or if it's in my head. I wasn't in the car for very long.

You have to find another way. You need to get out of here. Get the fuck out of your life.

I walk into the kitchen and stare at the knives, wondering how hard it would be to break the skin. Could I do it? I do it in my dreams all the time.

I can't.

You coward. Useless coward. Just do it.

No. No, please.

I have to get away from the voice.

Who, me?

My little sister Elly walks into the kitchen in her pajamas, oblivious to my shaking. She is humming the song she sang earlier that day, a cheery tune—music, to Elly, is life. Come Thou Fount.

I go downstairs to my room and sit on the closet floor, where I'm safe.

Drown yourself. Now's your chance. It would be easy. No one would notice the bath water running. I've thought about drowning before. After the initial strain of willpower, I bet it would feel nice and numb. *Oh yes. Nice and numb.*

I slam the door and curl into the fetal position, covering my ears with my hands. I don't want to listen.

You must get away. I'm staying right here. I'm not moving. *Oh, but you will. You have no choice. You're going to kill yourself tonight, and you have no way out. It's time to escape. It's time to*—**Come Thou fount of every blessing. Tune my heart to sing Thy praise.** Who do I listen to? Who do I listen to?

I'm safe inside my white-carpeted closet. I can just stay in here until the voice stops. But then I notice the long bar where all clothes are hanging. It wouldn't be very hard to hang myself. I imagine how it would feel, how my feet could dangle and my painted toes would hover over the ground. Would Mom find me first? *You know she would.* I don't want my mom to find me.

I spring from the floor and go upstairs. There's the sound of Dad with Elly in the kitchen.

He looks at me and asks if I'm okay, and I tell him I'm not. No, I'm not, Dad, no I'm not. I pace and then go up to the third floor, into my parents' room, and curl on their blue and white striped couch. Mom wakes up and turns on the light—she had gone to bed early. I squeeze my eyes against the light.

Bind my wandering heart to thee. *Fuck this.* Prone to wander, Lord, I feel it. **Come thou fount.** *What are you doing? You need OUT.* Please stop. **Of every blessing.**

My parents won't stop asking me questions.

"What's wrong?"

"Why are you acting like this?"

"Let us help you."

Mom is still in bed, confused, and Dad has his hands balled at his hips, looking at how I'm shaking. I can't answer. The voice is screeching at me, telling me to run. I don't want to run. I want to stay right where I am, safe, where I know I can't hurt myself. I sing to myself, the hymn over and over.

Run. RUN. GET OUT.

I must obey. I get up, ignoring my parents' confused questions, and put on Mom's fluorescent yellow running shoes by the door. Dad says he wants to come with me, and I don't want him to. While he puts on his shoes, I sprint for the stairs.

There are footsteps behind me on the road, loud. An army is following me. Thousands of people. This is why I must run. **Tune my heart to sing Thy praise?** Come thou *fuck fuck FUCK.* I am running because I have to. I am running because I must escape evil. And because someone is chasing me.

When my lungs start screaming, I fall, hard, on the road. I look and no one is behind me. Just Dad's idling car and his silhouette against the streetlight. He gets out of the car and comes over to me, helps me to my feet. I barely made it out of the neighborhood even though I felt like I'd run for miles.

"Let's get you home." Dad takes my hand and leads me to the car.

I can think once more. I need to go home. **Come Thou fount of every blessing, tune my heart to sing Thy praise.** There's a loud chorus in my ears.

∾

That night did not come out of nowhere, even though I thought it did. The two days prior to the incident, while my parents were still out of town, just days after England, found me bouncing around the house, packing and repacking for school, exercising in my room at two in the morning, calling Peter several times a day, and trying to ignore the voice in my head urging me to leave my life. I couldn't sleep. I was barely eating. And I was feeling a kind of happiness taking charge of my nerves. Mania is such a crazy beast—it's happiness and deadliness at the same time.

The voice was my own, but it wasn't. It was a demon, sort of, creating a desperate need—the illusion of a need—to "get out." That's what it was: Get out. Leave. Fly away. In my dreams, the only way to leave was to die, and that translated into escape in my awakened mind.

The fun and fast-paced months of my spring semester turned sinister. The overwhelming happiness turned against me. My frantic personality took over whoever was there before, going from fervent to uncontrollable to desperate.

The night I thought about killing myself? It was a long time coming. I snapped.

I told my parents I was fine. Just fine.

I told them the car incident was a weird little blip, that's all. I was leaving for school in three days, and I couldn't have been happier. I hadn't *really* wanted to kill myself, I said. That had been a weird night—that's all. I didn't even tell Peter.

My dad recognized it, of course. He didn't react too strongly, knowing he had to step carefully around my fragile state. So he followed me around for the remainder of my time at home, sitting with me in the afternoons as I painted my *masterpiece*. Greens, reds, and purples: the colors *spoke to me* and maybe, I thought, I was an artist at heart. It was a paint-by-numbers.

Dad gave me a pill so that I could sleep at night, and I did, without nightmares for the first time in months.

"Maybe you should spend some more time at home," he said the day before I left. He was treading lightly, hesitant to spook me into doing something rash.

"Why? I can't wait to see Peter."

He suggested that he drive the car out to Illinois with me, to help me get settled into the new apartment before classes started. The trip was long, but I slept for at least half of it, finally getting the rest I needed. My dad talked a lot about nothing, glancing over at me more than usual.

Leigha was glad I arrived early so that we could settle into our school apartment quickly. My dad did the heavy lifting and moving while Leigha and I sorted and organized. I told her that I'd kind of tried to kill myself, but I was fine now and it wasn't that big of a deal. I was excited to see Peter, and that was the most important thing. She reacted calmly, looking across the room at my dad instead of at me.

"So, Anna, I'm thinking about staying here for a little while." My dad and I were sitting in my living room, our feet propped up on boxes. Most of my stuff was unpacked, but we still had a little bit more to put away.

"Oh?"

"I want to hang out with you, if that's okay."

"Well, school doesn't start for a few days. And Peter won't get here for a while, so why not?"

"Maybe I'll stay a bit longer than that. And, actually, while I'm here, I thought we might visit a new doctor. Someone other than Dr. Hart. I made you an appointment."

I could tell he was still concerned about *that* night, but I was better. I'd just have to show him. "Fine, but I think everything is okay... I'll go if you want."

We went the following morning. Turns out he had made the appointment days earlier. Dr. Lowell was a petite woman immigrated from somewhere in Africa. I liked her accent and the smell of the cinnamon candle in her office. She asked me a lot of pointed questions, about my moods, the summer, the sleeping, and then turned to my dad.

"What have you observed?"

My dad looked at me—I was getting used to that—and then back to the doctor before he explained his own illness and my recent "behavior."

"I know the signs," he finished.

"So how many milligrams of—was it Lexapro?—are you taking?"

When I told her the amount, her jaw dropped.

"You're being overdosed," she shook her head. "You should *not* be taking that much."

"But that's how much Hart told me to take."

She shook her head again. "He is a *very* bad doctor. Can I talk to your dad alone for a few minutes?"

I waited outside the door, avoiding the secretary's eyes. Five, then ten, minutes. Finally, she invited me back in.

"Anna. I need to tell you this," Dr. Lowell placed her hand over mine. "I am going to diagnose you with Bipolar I disorder."

I saw Dad in the straitjacket. I saw Dad, tied to the bed.

"Your anti-depressant pushed you into a manic episode. Hypomania can be enjoyable, but it can become dangerous if it continues. We need you to stop the Lexapro as quickly as we possibly can." She spoke very slowly, enunciating every syllable. "It's going to take a while, and you'll have withdrawals, but we will have to find the right kind of medications that work with your body. I think you need to check into a hospital for a few days as a precaution."

"I am *not* going to a hospital. I am *not* doing that." I saw Dad locked in the thickly padded room.

"Well, I'm glad your dad is here then. If you don't want to be hospitalized, I want him to stay with you to monitor you. This is very important."

I agreed despite my uncertainty—it was too surreal to process—and listened as she prescribed two medications to start out with. She talked mostly to my dad, which relieved me. I didn't even know what to say.

❧

I tapped on the window of my apartment living room. "Rob!"

He waved, and I went outside to say hello.

"We're neighbors! I had no idea you'd be next door! Need help moving in?"

"No, I got it. Is that your dad?" He pointed at my car where my dad was unloading groceries.

I shrugged. "Long story."

"Okay, nice. Well, we should hang out soon."

I nodded, glad that he suggested it first, and left to help my dad unload. He'd insisted on cooking. Again. Hopefully Leigha wouldn't mind him hanging around so much. She was the only one I had told about the diagnosis, so she at least understood why he was here.

I stood back at the window and watched Rob carry boxes in from his own car, a small blue 1994 Volvo that had to be tight for his tall frame. What were the odds we'd live next to one another? Was I happy we'd be living so close? I needed to text Peter about dinner.

Peter arrived a few minutes later, giving me a quick kiss before greeting my dad. They did most of the chatting over the meal until my dad pointed at me with his fork. We'd talked about this earlier—how to bring it up— and my dad promised he'd help.

"Anna needs to explain some stuff." He dropped the burden entirely into my lap.

"What's wrong?" Peter asked.

"The doctor says I'm bipolar." There. It was out. That was simple.

"What?"

"I haven't been myself, lately. That's all. I guess I'm, you know, high or whatever. It's totally fine, though. Dad's going to be here for a while to help out, and I'm just going to go on with things as usual. Nothing is going to change."

Peter studied me. Nodded. "Okay."

"Do you understand?" Dad asked him.

"Yeah. But she's okay, right?" He wasn't asking me.

"I'm okay."

"Okay. Then it's okay."

Everything was okay. Peter thought so, I thought so. I didn't even need to think about the bipolar. The medication would work, and it would be okay.

And for the next few days, it *was*. I still felt happy. I hadn't snapped again like I'd done the week before. Classes started off well. Dad hovered, but not obnoxiously. And Peter was the perfect boyfriend again. He didn't mention the b-word, which was what I wanted. I was happy, he was happy, and everything was okay—until it wasn't.

~

The hallucinations started the night after my dad left to go home for a few days. I'd been doing well, and he had a few things to get done at work. I was in my room, getting ready for bed, and had just taken the pill that was supposed to help me sleep; it was a little blue pill, smaller than the tip of my thumb. I'd taken it before, but this time, my body's chemistry couldn't handle it. My brain defied me.

The room started waving. The air, that is. Up and down, up and down, all around. It felt neither cool nor hot, simply stale. I could feel it swaying, could see the particles moving and smiling at me and waving their fairy-like arms in my direction. Adrenaline kicked in; I scrambled into bed so that I wouldn't fall over, just like they tell you to do when you feel like you're going to faint.

I dialed his number slowly. I wanted to hear his voice.

Answer. Answer. Please answer.

Peter didn't answer.

Dad. Dad would still be awake. My fingers hovered over my phone's keys. They felt like inept logs of steel, heavy and unmoving. I couldn't move them. I couldn't move my fingers.

Numbers. And slowly, two more. My thumb dragged. Numbers. Oh, God. The last two.

"Hello?" Dad answered. He picked up on first ring.

"Help." My voice dragged out into a moan. My voice

sounded foreign. I couldn't form syllables. I couldn't remember how.

I looked towards the wall, where the sudden sound of screaming was coming from, in the corner of the room. They were screaming at me. "We're coming for you!" All those people on the wall. The picture frames wouldn't hold them for long. Leigha's mother's beautiful smile twisted into a wider sinister grin, her lips curling and stretching to the edges of the black frame. Her eyes roved over my entire body. Her straight teeth dripped into white pointed fangs, and her orange sweater lit on fire, burning the skin to flaky black pieces on her outstretched arm. Her fingertips touched the end of my nose.

"Anna? Did you hear me? Are you okay? Do you need help? What's wrong?" Did Dad hear the noises too?

"Hel...p. Something's not right. Not right, Dad. I took the pill. Just like you told me. They want me. Everyone. Everything..." I watched my sister pound against the glass, yelling at me. Her face was turned upside down. She was going to kill me. Her hands reached for me. The frame moved in and out around her body. "Revenge," she screamed. "Revenge!" She'd strangle me. Her long, hovering fingertips touched my throat.

"Is anyone there to help you? Hello? Are you at your apartment? Is Leigha there?"

"They're touching me! Everyone. They're after me. Help." I watched as more people came to life, shaking the frames that held them. They touched my hair, my ears, my tongue.

"Can you call Leigha? Is she around? Is she there?"

"No one." I began to cry. Was I crying? Nothing came out of my mouth.

"I'm calling Leigha. Hold on. I'm calling her right now. Okay? Just hold on."

I couldn't tell if I was screaming. Was I? I wanted to scream. I wanted to run. Leave my bed, leave my room. But my body wouldn't move. I was an anchor, wrapped around my bed sheets. I was shaking, but I wasn't moving. Move, move! My arms felt heavy, dead weight. They fell from my body. I dropped the phone.

I stared at the poster on my door in horror. It was moving too. An idyllic black and white scene of the Eiffel Tower burst into color. Greens and blues zig zagged away from the wall and up towards the ceiling fan. The reds and oranges swirled into spinning circles. The tower began to sway back and forth.

"Oh stop, please, no." The thought of it falling, crushing me, made me start laughing. Or crying? Laughing, crying, it didn't matter.

The tower began to crumble out of the poster. Chunks of red metal fell to the carpet with loud clangs. The pieces then fell sideways, aiming for my head but hitting the side of my bed instead. The bed shook. It was going to fall too.

"Anna!" A pounding at the door. "Let me in! You have to unlock the door!"

I don't remember anything else. They told me later that Leigha was home, that she hadn't heard my crying at first. I don't remember her holding me down in bed until my body stopped thrashing and fell into a disturbed sleep, but that's what she did. After talking to my parents on the phone about a medical oversight, a sleeping pill gone wrong, Leigha slept in the bed beside mine, not really sleeping.

∾

"Did something happen last night?" I walked into the kitchen the next morning. I had never experienced a hangover before, but I imagined that this was what it felt like.

"You don't remember?" Leigha looked at me like I had food on my face.

Images of a sinister smile and of a falling tower went before my eyes. "Oh..."

"Are you going to tell Peter? He should probably know what's going on."

I did tell Peter, later. I laughed my way through, trying to note every possible moment of hilarity. The stupid sleeping pill had messed with my mind.

Weird, right? How strange. What goofy dreams. Dad was coming back, but *that* would never happen again. Surely.

Peter placed his hand over mine and then fingers in my hair. He was *freaked out*, but we pretended he wasn't.

We made out that afternoon on my bed, frantic kisses an attempt to soothe nerves and begging for normalcy. The room did not move in and out this time. No one screamed from picture frames.

"You're fine," he said. His arms cradled my back against his chest.

"I don't think I am." I didn't say it out loud.

❦

A month and several different medications later, and I knew I was breaking. Each new pill brought on another ravaging effect on my body. My brain felt like it was sagging with effort. Would I be able to take this much longer?

One medication caused a burning restlessness—it felt like anxiety that refused me any peace. It was like I was wired and ticking before an explosion. I couldn't stop pacing about the apartment. My legs bounced beneath the tables in my classes, and I couldn't still the shaking in my hands. My fingers trembled so much that I couldn't hold onto my pens. I recorded lectures on my phone, unable to take my own notes.

I tried to make the excess energy funny. I would just work out with Peter more; the gym could be my outlet.

Dry mouth. Headaches. Nausea.

The worst was the lockjaw. I couldn't open my mouth more than two inches. Dad bought me a cork to stick between my teeth, but I couldn't bear it more than a few minutes. It ached until Dr. Lowell relented, switching me to another new bottle of pills.

I tried to normalize it. I told my friends that my dad was in town because of "family issues," not caring if they thought my parents were separated like it sounded. Dad just needed to spend time with me, I told them. I begged off of hangouts because of imagined chronic stomachaches. I forced myself on dates with Peter, and we laughed about all those silly medicines. I knew he sincerely wanted to help me; I just wouldn't let him.

I talked to Rob in passing. When my dad returned to Colorado again for a few days to take care of some business, I invited the entire England gang over. Only Rob came.

We sat over cups of coffee at the kitchen table. Indian summer had just begun, taunting us with our want for fall, so I had the air-conditioner on high and propped up a fan on the counter. I asked Leigha to stick around—I felt weird being alone with Rob without Peter knowing—but she left to study.

"So, how have you been?" I asked.

Rob smiled as he talked. He was graduating a semester early, so these were his last few months in college. He was eager to leave but had no idea what he was going to do next. What was one to do with an English major, anyway?

"And you?"

I was going to lie, like usual. I was fine, I was okay, and I was doing well. That's what I told everybody. But for some reason, I couldn't lie. Not to Rob.

I told him that life was hard. I wasn't doing well. I couldn't tell him why—too embarrassed—but said I was struggling. Didn't know how much more I could take. It was vague, but it was more than I told most people.

"Is that why your dad is around? I've noticed he's over a lot."

I nodded. "He's coming back tomorrow. He's going to take me to Michigan for a few days. I need time off from school. Staying at my uncle's."

"Sounds like you need it. Will Peter come?"

"Oh. No." I didn't want Peter to come.

"Are you going to be okay?"

"I hope so."

Rob didn't press me for more. I felt safe in our friendship. I'd confided more in him than I had in Peter, which gave me a little relief from being bottled up. I did feel a little bit guilty for talking to Rob, and not Peter. But I needed to be a good girlfriend—Peter didn't need to hear my problems.

"Do you have feelings for Rob?" Leigha asked me that night.

"What? Why would you say that?"

"Oh, I don't know. I thought maybe you did."

"I'm in love with Peter."

~

After our time in Michigan, I attended a half-day outpatient program at a day clinic. Dr. Lowell's idea, *not* mine. I walked up to the gray brick building with my arms crossed, throwing a dubious look back to my dad as he waited in the car. I'd try to last two weeks, attending the morning sessions before my school classes in the afternoon.

For the program, patients checked in at 8:00 and left at noon. It consisted of small group therapy, therapeutic lectures for the bigger group, and one-on-one meetings with a psychiatrist.

I hated it.

I hated the coordinator's big lips, how red they were without even a trace of lipstick.

I hated the patronizing. Cognitive Behavioral Therapy? Pure bullshit. I didn't need that.

I hated the ten-minute breaks, which meant I had to talk to people smoking on the patio who were *clearly* beneath me, or so I thought. An obese woman who couldn't stop crying about a divorce. A tattoo artist who wanted to kill herself. An older man who kept hitting on me.

I lasted three days. I was twenty; I could make these decisions for myself.

∼

I went to chapel for the first time in weeks. During the second worship song, I began to cry. Weep, really. I couldn't stop. The next song and the next and I couldn't stop myself, like a broken gushing faucet. The students in front of me glanced back several times, looks of pity and annoyance directed my way. I left halfway through the service and went back to the apartment to try to finish an assignment instead. This wasn't some spiritual experience. This was chemistry once again taking over.

I couldn't type the report. I stared at the screen, and the blinking cursor taunted me. I couldn't do it. I couldn't.

Everyone talks about pain after the fact. What was I supposed to do in the midst of pain, when I didn't know when the end would be? What could I tell myself, besides the pat answers, to get through it? It is so easy to look back at pain. To remember it, to recall. Yet I was looking at pain in the present. I was looking pain straight in the face, eye to eye, nose to nose. It was a staring contest. When would the pain blink?

"God, when will it be over?"

I have not forsaken you.

I dialed my dad, faster now, but just as difficult.

"I can't anymore. I have to go home."

My parents were more than supportive with me going home. It'd been their idea originally, and they were happy I came to the realization on my own. I deserved a break. I needed to rest. Come home, come home.

Peter sat on my bed next to me as I packed. I'd be back the next semester, so all I really needed to pack were my clothes. I could make the next day's flight with my dad. I knew I needed to leave. Still, I was ashamed of dropping out.

Peter and I were both crying. It was the first time we acknowledged what was happening, and we didn't know what else to do.

"I wish I could help you. But I can't."

"I know, Peter. I'm sorry."

"I don't know what to do."

"I know."

"God has a plan, Anna. He won't give you anything you can't handle."

"Yeah. Maybe."

"I love you."

"I know. I love you too."

We stayed together late into the night. Our kisses could make it better, I thought. He was my boyfriend—he wasn't going to leave me. I wasn't a crazy person. He loved me, didn't he?

~

The plan was for me to stay home for the rest of the semester, and then go back in January. The first couple of weeks were miserable. For the first week, I was either crying on the couch or pacing the floor.

But then, time at home became slow and sluggish. Medications were beginning to work, but it made the time feel arduous. No schoolwork meant I rested, but it also meant that I was bored. I cut my hair and dyed it red. I got a job selling elastic-waist pants to women over sixty, something supposed to make me feel purposeful.

I visited Jack at CSU, hoping to make use of an older friend. We spent an hour talking; bipolar never came up. I drove home realizing our friendship was over.

Peter and I talked almost every day and, like with Jack, anything related to the b-word never came up in our conversations. Bipolar didn't define me—I learned that trope quickly—so that meant we didn't have to talk about it.

"How are you doing?"

"Good! I'm working out again."

"Well, that's good."

"Yeah, totally good."

I assumed Peter didn't seem to want to talk about it. If he asked how I was feeling, it was always fine, fine, and fine. We had a normal relationship again: no more crying. He was the boyfriend, I was the girlfriend, and we were in love. Love meant that we were suited for one another, and we were. We got along extremely well, and I assumed that was because we were made for each other.

I think Peter would've talked about the bipolar if I'd let him. He cared. But I let our conversation fill with other things.

Mostly, I found comfort in my faith: I prayed constantly—throughout the day, as I'd done as a child. I didn't understand *why* God had let bipolar happen. What was the purpose? Was I supposed to learn something? *Not everything happens for a reason.* I'd considered that long ago.

But surely there was a reason. I *needed* there to be a reason. I was to become a better, stronger person. Bipolar wasn't part of the plan. It wasn't the *something better* God promised me, but maybe that was to come later. Maybe I had to go through something hard to reach that *something better?* Or, sometimes, did pain just happen with no reason at all?

I prayed for God's healing, and I got it—I don't think spiritual healing and the effects of medication are mutually exclusive. Side effects lessened and slowly, ever so slowly, I began to feel more like myself. Not the hyperactive me. Not the depressed me. The clear thinking me. My trust in God gave me peace; I gained confidence that I would, soon, feel completely better.

I relied on God through something difficult, and sanity was my reward. It made sense, and I would rely on that reasoning for as long as I needed to. I *needed* to believe this, even if it wasn't true.

I read the Psalms, over and over again.

> And those who know Your Name put their
> Trust in You

For You, O Lord, have not forsaken those
who seek You.

I am with you.

~

"Want more marshmallows?" Abby called to me
from her kitchen.

"Definitely," I called back. I leaned back into the
cushions and looked at the mess of paint tubes, glitter,
and canvases on the floor of her tiny apartment. She
desperately needed to vacuum.

My sister walked over to where I was sitting in front of
the TV, careful not to spill the two mugs of hot chocolate.

"Oh, and peanut butter?" I reminded her.

"Ah. Yes." She went back to the kitchen. We liked to
eat right from the jar with a shared spoon.

Abby and her husband, Randy, lived only ten minutes
from my parent's home. I think my sister felt sorry for me,
taking pity on the school dropout's sorry little life, and
she invited me over to her apartment in the afternoons to
watch *Gilmore Girls* and to eat too many snacks.

Abby and I weren't exactly close, but we weren't as
antagonistic as we'd been when I was in high school. She
had started a peace treaty of sorts when she asked me to
be her maid of honor a year earlier.

"How are you feeling today?"

"Down."

She winced. "Sorry."

Over the course of those few months, I confided in

Abby about my health, and she reciprocated by buying more mini marshmallows. An hour in the afternoon turned into three, then four.

I knew Abby suffered from some depression too, but she didn't talk much about it, unlike me. Her chronic migraines prevented her from holding a job, and, when she wasn't in bed with an aura, she spent a lot of her time painting scenes of outer-space on large canvases in her kitchen or working on a young adult sci-fi novel.

Seeing her in her everyday life, curled in pain on her couch or on the floor with the lights off, helped me understand that her pain was more real than I'd imagined. Migraines aren't just headaches. I felt guilty for not having much compassion in the past and was determined to empathize.

We were two very different people, but I thought our illnesses gave us something in common: life, not as we planned. I just hoped that bipolar wouldn't be as debilitating as migraines.

≈

I don't remember how the fight started, but there we were, in my parents' kitchen, screaming at each other. My entire family planned to go out to dinner together, but we never made it out the door. What did I say that triggered such a response from Abby? I wish I could remember. I wish I could know what provoked such anger—how long had it been simmering beneath the surface of marshmallows and peanut butter?

I don't know how it started, but it was a fight between

all of us. We were all yelling. Abby, Mom, Dad, the others, all standing there, in the kitchen.

My younger sisters were upset about my parent's special treatment of me; I was mad that any of them dare be upset; my parents were defensive; I thought they weren't defensive enough.

"You're the favorite," one of them said. "You took Mom and Dad away from us with all your problems."

What did my sisters mean? I'd taken Mom and Dad away? What did they mean I'd been all my parents cared about?

"She needed us," Dad tried to explain, "Don't get her worked up too much."

"Shut up, Dad," I didn't want him talking about me like I wasn't there.

"We were here for you all," Mom tried, pleading with them.

"You were there for *her*."

"I hate you!" I screamed the words, hating that I also started to cry. I didn't want what she said to be true. I didn't want my parents to feel bad for helping me.

I didn't care what the others said—it was Abby I was mad at. Just because she stood there, defending the others instead of me.

So, the last few months, the TV and the conversations, that was a farce? Had she been feeling this about me that entire time, biding her time until she could make me feel terrible? I thought we were friends.

"I hate you!" I took Mom and Dad away from the rest of my family? "I hate you. I never want anything to do with you ever again." My words sounded calculated, but they weren't.

"Calm down." Dad knew this wasn't going to resolve well.

"No! Tell me I'm a burden. Go on, tell me." I looked at Abby only.

I feared that they really *did* think I was a burden, that they had felt that all along. I couldn't be alone in this. I needed them. I needed them to understand that I never meant to make it hard for any of them.

Mom sighed heavily. "She's not my favorite. She just needs the most help right now."

"Get the hell away from me." I couldn't be around them anymore—especially Abby. Abby was supposed to stand up for me when all of the others didn't.

I waited for the tears to stop and then looked straight at her, this time crafting the words and then saying them as slowly and as coldly as I could, "Abby, I never want to talk to you again. You. Are. No. Sister. To. Me."

I knew it was a mistake as soon as I said it. Abby never said that I was a burden... I'd just felt like she had. I swallowed instant regret and walked away, not listening to my parent's pleas to come back to work things out. We didn't talk for the rest of my time at home.

~

Rob and I started texting. After I'd been home for a few weeks, he reached out, asking me if I was okay. It felt nice to be noticed, to be missed. I wrote to him in detail, telling him everything that had happened

to me: the bipolar, the suicide stuff, and the hallucinations.

We started one of those conversations that don't really
end. It was sort of like an email exchange in text form,
simply going back and forth over an extended period of
time, always picking up wherever it left off.

I felt guilty, just as I had in England, like I was doing
something behind Peter's back. We were just talking,
nothing more, but I knew it meant more to me than it
should. I kept hoping that Rob would suddenly and out
of nowhere declare feelings for me.

If Rob told me he liked me, then I would break up
with Peter. But I didn't want to ruin a perfectly good relationship for nothing. Peter was a good boyfriend; he'd
done nothing wrong. I loved him—we got along so well
—only because he was a part of the plan.

~

I told my mom about my confusion one night in the
living room. We were cozy, in blankets and by the
fireplace. We watched the snow fall from the window and
accumulate on the patio.

"There's just something about Rob. I can't explain it.
But I love Peter." I picked at a thread in the pillow.

"How do you know you love him?"

"Because I like being with him. He's so sweet. And he
hasn't broken up with me through all this bipolar stuff—I
couldn't possibly break it off after that."

"You don't owe him anything, Anna."

I didn't say anything. I felt like I *did* owe him.

"Why don't you make a pros and cons list?"

Typical organized Mom. Too pragmatic. But, hey, not a bad idea. I got up and grabbed a sheet of notebook paper before settling back down into the armchair. I wrote a few lines, paused, tapped my pen against the page, and wrote a few more.

Rob pros:

- We had things in common. He made me laugh. I couldn't stop thinking about him.

Rob cons:

- I didn't know how *he* felt.

Peter pros:

- Our relationship was sweet; it was comfortable. He was a perfectly good boyfriend. He treated me well. We got along.

Peter cons:

- There was something missing.

Peter invited me to Jersey for a weekend in late November. A friend was getting married. I took my time packing, trying to find the perfect dress that would make me look thin. I needed to be confident, and, back then, thin equaled confident.

On the plane, I thought about how to breakup—what to say, when to say it—and wrote down several versions on airline napkins. A wedding wasn't the ideal time to break up with someone, but I didn't want to do it over the phone.

But the kissing was too nice. His embrace was comforting and made me think I was making a mistake. There was nothing wrong with Peter. He was attentive, kind, and easygoing. Love meant sticking by someone through something hard, and he hadn't broken up with me after the breakdown, had he? Sure, we didn't talk about it much, but he never walked away. Love meant I liked being with him. Love was mutual attraction, and we had that. Maybe it wasn't the love I'd always dreamed about, but it was enough. I slept on the plane ride home.

I confided in Rob about my doubts, the only thing we talked about that was probably too personal. I kept hoping that he would, maybe, try to persuade me to break up. He didn't. He took a balanced view, encouraging me to trust my feelings. *Not* what I wanted him to say. I wanted him to tell me exactly what my—his—feelings were.

I decided I would continue to love Peter: it was a conscious decision. We'd date and then we'd marry, like good Christians are supposed to do. Rob was just a leftover thing of the summer's mania, a flight of fancy. A close friend. I needed to distance myself from him.

Why did I think I could make a "decision" to love someone? I didn't understand that it needed to be organic, natural. It needed to be "from the heart," not the head.

A week before I was to return to school, Rob sent me a paper he'd written for his senior seminar. Apparently, he'd written about me, and he wanted to make sure I was okay with it.

In the paper, Rob talked about literature, pain, and faith and how those intertwined in his life. He wrote about his reaction to my breakdown. He was deeply affected by my experience and felt even more about our friendship than I hoped.

Did this mean he had feelings for me? I didn't know. I wanted it to mean that he had feelings, I really did. But I loved Peter. Sort of.

~

I unpacked my sweaters, jeans, and books in a hurry, making sure I left half of the dorm closet empty for Elizabeth. Leigha was studying abroad for the spring semester, so my friend Elizabeth and I were now roommates. I didn't know how we'd get along sharing a space —no one was like Leigha.

I spent the rest of the afternoon primping, knowing Peter would appreciate how sculpted my shoulders were from working out. I was nervous to see him again. Nervous and happy. This was a new start. We'd dream about the future, talk about the new semester. Maybe I'd even tell him about Abby. My bipolar was under control —we didn't even have to talk about it—and since I was taking a light course load, the two of us would have plenty of time to catch up on our love for one another.

Of course, I didn't anticipate that he'd break up with me.

I couldn't have been more surprised or more humiliated. There I was, planning and trying to be in love more than ever, and he was telling me he didn't love me anymore.

"I'm sorry."

"Did I do something wrong?"

"No. It's just not there."

It was embarrassing the way I started crying, blubbering in front of him. We were supposed to be in love.

He didn't say anything about the bipolar. He didn't have to.

But maybe that's not fair. Maybe bipolar had nothing to do with it. I can't know.

We got back together a few days later. I suggested we try it again, just to see and to ease my humiliation. He agreed, but when he didn't show up to the birthday party some of my friends surprised me with, I knew it was over. We broke up again, and I began to question if it had been love after all. I prayed about it, confused.

God, what are You doing? I thought Peter was part of the plan.

For I know the plans I have for you, plans for hope and a future.

10

_____

He loves me. He loves me not. He loves me?

I was driving the two hours to Rockford to meet up with Rob, a place halfway between our homes. I don't think I was paying much attention to the road. I'm a safe driver, and when I'm absentminded, I tend to drive exceedingly slow. It took me a little longer to get there than I'd planned.

I'd left early, though; I was too anxious to lie around the apartment in the outfit I'd picked out days before. I didn't need an outfit that made me look skinny; Rob didn't care about that sort of thing. Still, I wanted to look pretty, and I picked a sweater that would match my eyes.

I wanted him to like me. I'd wanted it for a long time. Why did I feel so ashamed of that? It'd only been a month since I'd cried over Peter. Was I using Rob to feel better about myself?

No. I had had feelings for Rob before the breakup. Even in England.

Even in England? Yeah, he'd never been just a friend.

I drummed my fingers faster on the steering wheel, out of sync with the radio's rhythm.

Did that count as cheating? I really didn't want it to. I wasn't "that kind of girl." I wasn't. I needed to see the guy I couldn't stop thinking about.

I debated about a potential hug. Yes or no?

I arrived, parked, and found a coffee shop and bought us two large black coffees—just as he liked it. I waited a while; his mug went cold. He was late (stuck in traffic), and the woman behind the counter smiled sadly and said she didn't think he was coming. It was five; she needed to close the shop now. She was short and round with grandma curls and pink glasses—didn't think he was coming?—grandma or not, I hated her for even suggesting it.

We met outside (no hug), and he suggested dinner quickly.

"I know the perfect place."

"Oh?" I wondered if he had planned it.

We sat in the brick alcove inside the small Italian restaurant, and I was glad that the food took a long time to arrive. He was even taller than I remembered, 6'5." In my memories from England, he was skinny and lanky, but there in Rockford he was fuller, broader. Every evolutionary instinct was in his favor in that regard, like I could sense his mating skills without even trying. I kept noticing the blonde hair on his thick wrists and forearms.

Conversation was easy, as natural as I'd hoped: family life, my schoolwork, his so-far-fruitless job search. I told him my hopes to backpack Europe, and we acted like it was an original idea. He told me about the nonexistent job offers, and we acted like it was unusual. Dinner came and went. We both leaned forward in our chairs, elbows on table, hands almost touching.

I surprised myself when I started talking about the bipolar. I liked to pretend that it never happened. It wasn't a big deal. It wasn't a big deal. Bipolar didn't define me. I told myself that a lot. Life goes on; I'd only grown stronger.

But with Rob, I found myself describing some of the side effects, some of my frustrations with being stuck at home. Bipolar was *hard*.

"How did it affect your faith?" He was the first friend to ask me that, the first not to immediately quote a Bible verse about the value of suffering.

"Well, I had this dream a while back..." I surprised myself again. I described the vision I'd experienced as a teenager, the dream that I remembered so vividly.

"...And it was God's voice saying: I have something better for you." I looked at him, wary of any disbelief on his face. "I've had a lot of different kinds of dreams. Even lucid dreaming. Trust me, I have. This one was different. I think it was a vision."

"What do you think it means?" His eyes were wide, his expression soft. He believed me.

"I don't know exactly. I've been trying to figure that out for the last few years. God has been faithful thus far. He really has. I mean, look at me now. Healed."

But healed for how long? I changed the subject quickly, jumping back to his job search. As he spoke, I looked at the small, raised mole at the corner of his top lip and wondered, briefly, what it would be like to kiss him there.

We talked until the restaurant closed and parted with promises to see each other again. (This time, a hug.)

I called my mom on my drive home. This was the kind of thing Mom loved. She was the only one who knew about my former feelings about Rob, the one who suggested the pro and con list in the first place.

"I think he likes me. I think."

"So he paid for your meal."

"Yeah."

"You talked a long time."

"Yeah."

"Good eye contact and all that."

"Yeah."

"You like him."

"Yeah."

"Well. I guess you'll have to wait and see."

"But, Mom, this is going to drive me crazy."

"...Yeah. Me too."

Rob texted me the next day, asking if he could come down and take me out for Valentine's Day. I considered this pretty bold, because he was usually so shy. I had never had a Valentine before.

My roommate, Elizabeth, was worried he was a rebound. I told her I'd be careful, knowing it wasn't what she said. She tried to be happy for me, keeping the peace in our new roommate relationship.

The night he drove down from Wisconsin, the night before Valentine's Day, Rob and I watched a movie and then talked on the couch. I wondered if we'd address the obvious.

Bring it up. Bring it up. Bring it up. I felt foolish, girlish, the way I wanted him to tell me he liked me. I knew he did, given that we were going out for Valentine's Day, but I wanted it said out loud. I wasn't sixteen, but I felt like it.

"So. What is this exactly? This." I gestured to the space between the two of us.

"I like you."

It felt good to hear the words I craved. (He loves me!) There. Sixteen-year-old me taken care of. I don't remember what I said exactly, but it was along the lines of, "I fell for you in England, and I haven't gotten up yet."

We talked about it for a while, a long while, how we could try to meet up when we could. His grandmother lived near campus, and he could stay with her when he came to visit. We could make it work.

I kept looking at his lip mole.

∾

I was happy. Not happy in a manic way but happy in a way that made me feel genuine. It was less exciting than Amsterdam and England but better because it was *real*. We were able to build on the friendship that was already there.

Rob moved down to his grandmother's house, only a ten-minute drive from campus. He could job search on his computer from anywhere, he said, and may as well be by me. Besides, he liked the Chicago area. He got a part-time job at a sandwich shop, humiliating for a proud college graduate, but necessary to pay for gas.

When I got into a small car accident during a snow-storm I shouldn't have been driving in, Rob picked me up from the hospital— the ambulance ride was my overreac-tion to a bloody nose and airbag—and we spent the next few hours huddled in the backseat of his own car on the side of the road because of the road conditions, watching *Star Wars* on his laptop. It was cold; it was bliss.

"You can hold my hand if you want," I said, pulling the blanket closer to my chest. I kept my eyes on the computer screen as I said it.

"I *guess* I will." He smiled.

Snow covered the windows, leaving us in our own special cocoon. There was something romantic about being trapped in a storm together, and I couldn't stop grinning.

The resulting concussion, making its presence known over the next few weeks, made it difficult to read for class. Rob helped me with my homework, reading aloud as I leaned on his shoulder or put my head in his lap. I loved the way he stroked my hair, like the way my mom had done when I was younger.

If I wasn't in class, I was with Rob. Overnight, I disap-peared from my friend group. The only one who really saw me was Elizabeth, in the mornings in the bathroom or in-between classes while Rob was making subs.

One night, when Rob had a rare evening shift, Eliza-beth and I went out for dinner at our favorite Thai place a few blocks away from the apartment. We sat at the small, sticky, black table, making small talk and waiting for our meals.

"Do you ever hang out with that group of friends anymore?" She playfully attacked her noodles with her chopsticks.

"Not really anymore..." I looked down at my own plate.

"You're okay with that?"

"I mean, I guess. They don't really like Rob."

"Oh, c'mon."

"Okay, maybe it's not that they don't *like* him."

"They don't know him."

"Exactly. They all said he's a rebound I'll regret." I remembered that one girl had reprimanded me quite harshly, telling me I'd made an outright mistake, and I couldn't forgive her for not understanding.

"I don't think he's a rebound."

"You did at first." I tried not to make it an accusation.

"Well." She took a bite. "I trust you."

"What am I supposed to say to them? That I'd liked Rob *during* my relationship with Peter, so it's okay? They're friends with Peter. I don't want to embarrass him."

"Sounds like *you're* embarrassed."

I shrugged. "They can think whatever they want. I don't care." I took a vicious bite of my rice.

My dad told me that, even though I was over Peter, *he* was not. He tried to make it seem like he was joking. My mom gave me the green light, as did Leigha when she Skyped me from where she studied abroad in Italy. I valued their opinion more than others'. But I probably would have dated him regardless.

~

We spent countless hours in his grandma's basement.

We hunched over our laptops at the same time. I worked on homework, and he did freelance work.

We watched shows and played cards on his bed like two old people in a nursing home.

We read aloud to each other. Dostoyevsky (Rob's choice) and Don DeLillo (mine).

We made pancakes and spaghetti for dinner, over and over and over. I didn't care if I gained back the weight I'd lost, because Rob didn't.

We talked about the bipolar now and then like it was a thing of the past, nothing powerful enough to disrupt our happiness.

We talked about literature and social justice. We were well-intentioned pseudo-intellectuals, stereotypes in our early twenties.

I asked him to kiss me, and he did. He asked me to kiss him again, and I did.

Those two months felt like years.

One night when we talking in his car, he told me he was falling in love with me. It was too soon, I thought. So, of course, I told him I felt the same way.

Over my spring break, I went on a cruise in Barbados with Elizabeth and her parents. It was a spontaneous thing but turned out to be one of the most relaxing vacations of my life. The water, the sun, the sand—it was just like the brochure promised.

I had time to think by myself, tanning up on the deck in the warm sunshine. I burned the back of my legs—the burn left an actual scar on my thighs—as I stared at the same page in my book for an afternoon, thinking about what Rob had said.

Was it too soon? Everything was going so fast, and my feelings were so strong. I knew what I felt was different from what I'd felt with Peter, though I couldn't articulate how, except to say my feelings for Rob were more authentic—not contrived.

I wanted to know what God thought. I wanted His approval. *If this is of You, bless it.* That's what I prayed the night we started dating, an early plea for clarity. Rob had told me that he was praying the very same thing.

"God, is this of you? Do I love him?" I prayed it over and over.

Rob.

"Is this real?"

Rob.

I trusted what I recognized as God's voice: it was the assurance I needed and wanted. God was not just telling me to date him—He was telling me that Rob was the one. It was made so clear to me, so obvious. I know that may sound unbelievable, and that's probably because it *is* unbelievable. Rightly so. But I just *knew.* I distinguished God's prompting from all the other rambling thoughts; it was the voice I recognized from childhood. Rob was the one, and he was different from all the rest. Maybe I should have had doubts, but I knew we'd be holding hands at sixty-five.

When I got back from the trip, I told Rob I wasn't just falling. I was in the sticky sweetness of love, the kind that would leave a permanent stain if ever it left.

~

A few months later, I was in the Bakersfield airport, waiting for Rob. I had seamlessly finished my junior year of college and transitioned into an administrative internship in my California hometown, living at the house of family friends, playing dress-up in heels and a pencil skirt and making endless trips to the copy machine. I wasn't sleeping well, which was reminiscent of the year before, but why worry when Rob was coming?

I planned to drive him around my town for nostalgia's sake, and then we'd drive over to the coast and stay at my grandparents' place. I tried not to hope for a ring but hoped anyway. I wanted him to ask me to marry him. We'd both hinted. Things had progressed at record speed, but I knew our faith was at the center of it, and I wasn't afraid.

Romance happened a little differently in my tiny Christian world. Rob and I never thought to move in together when we knew we loved one another; we made a bigger commitment than that. I believe marriage is sacred; *two shall become one* is an ancient and beautiful sacrament that can last despite cultural changes. But only if I wanted it to.

Others don't understand, and that's okay; they can see

it as outdated if they want, but I'd like to replace their mockery with respect.

I was young, almost twenty-two, but I wasn't afraid to get married. The only thing I feared was people's judgment. Too young. Too naïve. Too Christian. I couldn't help being a bit defensive. I still can't.

I knew we'd change and continue to figure out who we were (I knew we wouldn't be the same people at fifty as we were at twenty), but I wanted to transition and change together, not apart. I still needed to grow up, but I wanted to start my life with someone. Popular American culture has made the two mutually exclusive when, maybe, they don't have to be.

I wasn't afraid of commitment. Why would I be, when I could follow those who had gone before me? My great-grandmother got married at seventeen and stood by her husband through the Depression, wars, and illness until he died. My grandfather got married at nineteen and, even on days he really didn't *like* her, he fell in love with his wife again and again. My parents got engaged after just six weeks of dating and are still committed to one another, going on thirty years. These were the only role models I grew up with.

Maybe it's because they're all lucky; maybe it was something strange and spiritual. I know divorce is sometimes an inevitable reality. Of course it is. But the people before me told me that love and marriage go hand in hand, that you can love someone even when you don't feel like it anymore, and *what therefore God has joined together, let not men put asunder.* And I believed them.

So, when Rob asked me to marry him a few days later, I said yes.

Before the proposal, we spent the entire day at the beach. We bought sunglasses and ice cream cones, walked the pier, ate fish in an expensive restaurant. (Sappy and wonderful.) I slipped a pink sundress over my swimsuit when it got cool, and we walked to a secluded area where giant rocks jutted out of the wet sand around us.

At sunset, he handed me a long poem he'd spent weeks writing.

...Sing to me your eyes...

I looked up from the paper, and he was kneeling.

⁓

"Bipolar has a funny way of showing up at very inconvenient times." My flight from California had arrived just a few hours earlier.

"It's okay," Rob said, rubbing my arm. We were sitting on the floor of my bedroom as I unpacked my suitcase.

"It's just a blip. Nothing full-blown."

A blip, just something to remind me that, yes, bipolar was still hovering about my brain, something I couldn't completely forget.

It was a few weeks after the proposal, and I rarely slept. When I did sleep, I wet the bed during one of many lucid night terrors. My mind raced at work; I went through things feverishly; anxiety kept me from leaving my car. I faked ease as long as I could before I had to return home early, embarrassed at my apparent lack of capability. Would I ever be able to hold a job when it seemed to so easily tip me off the edge? I didn't see my anxiety as a symptom of mania, just thought it was a side effect of a medication.

"I just didn't want to have to change meds."

"They'll help." Rob grabbed a few shirts and started to help me fold. "I'm just glad I'm here until you leave for school."

Rob had just moved to Colorado for a new job and planned to keep me company for the rest of summer as best he could, trying to make me smile when I couldn't.

"I'm not moving back the wedding date."

"I know. You told me already."

"I just want to make it clear."

"It's clear."

"I just want to *feel* better."

"It's fine, sweetie. Fine. I promise it will be fine."

Even when I sank into a mini, two-week depression, Rob assured me that everything would be fine (fine, sweetie, fine), that the upcoming semester would be easy, and that graduating early was a good idea, just as I'd told him weeks earlier.

I *did* feel better, and I took on an 18-credit course load so that, by January, I'd be done with school and be able to get married.

During the fall, I Skyped Rob every night, eager to hear about his life, as he was now living in my parents' basement and standing in front of a bunch of high school juniors each morning, begging them to *at least try* to care about Hamlet. The first year of teaching is tough. My own classes were good, I told him, and I enjoyed having Leigha, back from her study abroad, at school. Nothing unusual.

I didn't tell him about the racing and obsessive thoughts or early morning sleepless hours. Or that I ignored the new "escapist thoughts" that had already come knocking at my mind. *I* wasn't noticing them for what they were. I should have, but maybe delusion had already set in, keeping me from seeing what was happening. Mental illness distorts reality.

I became, once again, preoccupied with my looks, to the point of unnatural obsession. (Another sign of bipolar that I didn't understand?) And that voice was there again, telling me things that made absolutely no sense.

You're hideous.

Get out.

Get out of what? My perfect life? I didn't need out of anything.

Get out.

I slipped into class late. Late a lot these days. But it didn't matter, did it? I was going to be the next Bill Gates. I had a gift from God—me, a freaking genius. It made me feel proud and special, like I was winning something.

I yawned, trying to focus on my professor. I didn't really feel tired, but my body felt heavy in my chair. I'd been staying up late on my computer, unable to sleep.

When class was over, I left, eager for a cappuccino. I went from the building with a small refrain pounding in my head. *Get out. Leave your life. GET OUT.* The thoughts consumed me, swirling before my eyes when I sat at my desk, stood before the mirror, went out with friends. Wherever I went, the thoughts followed.

I began to feel detached from myself, like an observer. I left my mind and my body and became someone else.

～

I am sitting in my senior seminar days later, and my leg is moving up and down. I can't sit still anymore. My knee hits the table again and again, and the girl next to me looks over, annoyed. Her look tells me I'm jiggling the table.

She's annoyed? I'm annoyed. I'm annoyed because I am here and because I'm not away and because I'm here. I can't get out. *Fuck this. You need out.*

My professor is talking about something. Her mouth opens and closes, but I can't hear. I don't care what she's saying. *I'm a fucking genius.* I'm getting out of here. Away, away. Why? Why do I want to leave? I don't know—do I have to know? I don't know anything. *You want to be free, that's all, free. What's the harm in that?* Rob will understand. *He'll get it.* No, he won't. He won't get it at all. *But that's okay, he will.*

But where can I go? *Go anywhere.*

Amsterdam. A plane ride away. That's freedom. I like biking. Biking, free, laughing, laughing on bikes. Freedom. *Go to Amsterdam. Now. Go.*

I pull my phone out of my bag and look at it under the table. My professor sees—it's obvious—*who gives a shit?* I find an airline, a flight that leaves in a few hours.

That's doable. Five thousand dollars for a first-class seat. *That's nothing.* I think I might have five thousand dollars in my bank account. *Probably.*

I think about what I'll pack. Sweaters? Is it cold yet? I'll pack some red lipstick. I haven't worn lipstick in a long time. *Men like lipstick.* Does Rob? *Doesn't matter. You're going to be free.*

I enter my credit card information.

But wait. I think of my passport, inside the small safe in my parents' closet.

It's okay. We'll think of something else.

My professor is talking about something remarkably stupid. I don't need this crap. I'm a *fucking genius.*

Where can I go? *You need out.* Where can I meet men? Where is somewhere no one will find me?

New York City. Why not? Random and perfect and random. *Freedom awaits.*

I find a new flight, enter my card info, and click. First class, 3A. I pick up my things and leave the class. My backpack bumps against the girl next to me. She looks at me, furious.

I run back to my apartment. As fast as I can, because I'm in a race for freedom and for I don't know what.

I have ten minutes to pack. *Hurry.* I am hurrying. I will be seductive. I will charm them all. I grab the black dress that is sort of too short and a pair of red heels that I've worn twice. A purple thong and no bra. *They'll want you.* I know. I throw makeup and a toothbrush into the duffle, look at the pill case on my desk and decide to leave it there. I need freedom from the oppression. *You need out.*

I can't drive fast enough. There's a refrain in my head. *Self-destruct. Self-destruct. Escape.*

But Rob?

He won't want you anymore. I don't want to hurt him. *So end it.* I don't want to hurt him. *Self-destruct.* But—*self-destruct. If you ruin yourself, he won't want you. You'll be free.*

I call him on speakerphone. He answers—I don't know why, because he's at work—and I tell him I'm leaving.

"What are you talking about? Are you okay? You sound funny."

"It's over."

"What is?"

"I'm going to be free."

"Free?"

"I'm leaving and I'm not coming back and I'm saying goodbye forever. Trust me, you'll want this. You don't want me. I'm going to find other men."

"Where are you?"

...

"Where are you?"

"I'm almost at the airport."

"Don't go anywhere. You're not being rational. You need to calm down. Something isn't right. You're going to hurt yourself."

"Goodbye, Rob." I hang up. *Free at last.*

He calls. Calls again. I turn my phone off.

I arrive at O'Hare and try to find a parking space. I've never parked in the outside lot, but today it seems like a good idea. I park, turn my phone on, see nine missed calls, and check the status of my flight. The flight information on my app is gone. I know that Rob managed to cancel my flight. He knows my passwords.

He's sabotaged you. It's over. He wants to defeat you. He wants to cage you in.

"How dare you," I say to Rob when he picks up on the first ring.

"I'm coming to you. I'll be there in a couple hours. Please be safe. Don't go anywhere."

"Fine." *What are you doing? You need out.* I don't want to leave anymore. *But.*

"So you'll stay there?"

"I'm going downtown. I'm going to get lost." *Better than nothing.* I hang up.

I drive from O'Hare to Michigan Ave and then to a part of the city I've never been to before. The morning sinks into the afternoon as I walk the streets. I'm caught by how happy the sky looks. It's blue—it's never this blue —and it's all for me. The sky knew I needed it to be blue today, didn't it?

I meander in and out of shops. I look at lamps. Maybe I'll get a lamp. Or a slutty nightgown. I buy clothes. I look at the large, rounded breasts on the mannequins. I could use a boob job. Or a lamp.

It all makes sense. I don't know why my mom keeps trying to call me. Why did Rob talk to her? Can't they see my logic is sound? All I want is to be free from my life. I want to be happy again. Carefree. I'll walk around until I'm free.

My mind quiets, and I'm bored. I call my mom back.

"Just go somewhere safe. Check into a hotel and stay in the room, okay? Rob will be there soon." She knows that this is different from the last time. This time, I'm alone. This time, I'm older and will be more drastic. This time, I'll kill myself. "The important thing is that you're safe. That's all I want for you, honey."

Honey, don't you dare. Honey, don't listen to her.

"Okay." Why do I agree? Maybe she's right. Maybe something's off. "Okay, I will."

"Text Rob when you get there. He'll meet you there when his flight gets in."

You're ruining the plan. What plan? *Don't you want to be free?*

I do as she says, and I wait for Rob at the hotel. How much time has passed? *Waiting, waiting. Always waiting. Don't you want to live to your full potential? You need out. So, go on. Do it.*

Hurt yourself. That doesn't make sense. *Oh, yes it does. You know it does. The blood will be a sign of change. It will help you leave. Do it. Self-destruct.*

I lie on the floor and move my arm back and forth on the edge of the room's air-conditioning unit. Scratches. *Not enough.* Rob is almost here. I break a glass cup in the sink. Blood on my arms. On my fingers. I stare at the shards in the sink. They're menacing. *Out, get out.*

Rob is here, and he is with me—he's here from the airport, and I can tell he is scared. Don't be scared, Rob. Everything is okay. *Fuck this*—shut up, stop talking, because Rob is here now. And it's okay, and he is with me. His presence soothes me. We sit on the bed and we talk and my mind quiets again and he is with me. Let's go to dinner, he says. Okay, I say. We sit across from each other and eat pasta. I laugh—how funny this all is—and he touches my hand, and I laugh some more. Well, that was weird, wasn't it? I'm fine now.

He wants to stay the night with me, to make sure I stay fine. We watch a show and then another and then he holds me in bed as I try to fall asleep. He holds me tightly, too tightly lest he lose me. I think of how I've dreamed of spending the night together, and it wasn't like this at all. In that daydream, we're making love for the very first time, and he is happy. In that daydream, he's so happy to be by me, to be touching me. But he's not happy right now. He's holding me to stop me from hurting myself. How funny.

Then it is 2:00 a.m. and I am wide-awake and his breathing tickles my neck. *Now it's time. Get out. Do what you have to do.* I wriggle out of his arms and out of bed. Go into the bathroom. How can I get out? *Bang bang bang.* There is blood on the bathroom counter. It doesn't hurt enough. *Bang bang bang.* Blood in my eyes. Then Rob is here, pulling me away from the wall. We fight. He wrestles me down, pins my arms to my sides. It hurts. He's crying and begging me to stop. He holds me until my breathing finally slows.

We take a walk outside. Fresh air will do us good, surely. But I'm running away from him and into trees *bang bang bang.* I lose him. *Free at last.* He finds me banging repeatedly into a telephone pole.

Time to go to the hospital.

∾

I don't like to think about the night Rob had me admitted, the night where I had to squat naked before a nurse so she could check for weapons in my vagina. I don't like to think about the hospital at all. But I do every now and then, if only to remind myself that it really happened.

I know mental institutions have come a long way. The doctors and nurses care about the patients; the therapists go out of their way to befriend people, to coax them out of their rooms and into group activities. They do everything they can to protect patients from themselves as humanely as possible. Being in that environment made hurting myself an impossibility, which, I suppose, is the whole point.

But that hospital still remains a lurid memory.

I met with a psychiatrist only twice. She assessed me within minutes, taking me off medications and then assigning me to a new drug for the rest of my life. I prayed for a placebo to kick in quickly—the doctor said a placebo effect was perfectly fine, as long it made me feel better. The medicine would take its time. All I wanted was to stop the rapid pacing in my head, that driving urge to flee from here, there, anywhere. Anywhere meaning, of course, nowhere.

I hated the necessary condescension of the nurses and therapists. The nurses asked me about bowel movements in front of others, wouldn't let me shut the door while I peed, made me hand over my plastic silverware after eating, rapped on the plastic Velcro shower doors if they hadn't heard from me in a while.

Therapists insisted upon inane group activities that reminded me of grade school. Nothing was required, but if I missed an activity—be it music therapy with tambourines or sessions where we listed ten positive things about ourselves—they'd tell my therapist, who was in control of my discharge, that I seemed withdrawn, still not well. It didn't matter that my body was wracked with side effects; I *needed* to talk about *mindfulness.* The overused therapy buzzword. Mindful of what? My misery? I *still* hate that word.

I wasn't strapped to a bed like my father had been in the 90's. Maybe I wasn't that much of a danger to myself after all. Did I need to be there in the first place? It was an insult to my intelligence. I felt *watched.* To be subject to people I didn't know telling me exactly how I felt and exactly what I should be doing at any given moment felt humiliating.

I despised the other patients. They were beneath me, so beneath me. I hated the way they were so typical of mental patients, crying and whining and groaning or creeping around like shadows. What stereotypes. *I* wasn't like them.

I couldn't see that I needed to be in a mental hospital just as much as the others. I let myself feel superior to suppress my humiliation. I was in a manic episode, yet there I was, thinking myself the sane one.

I hated the way we all wore pajamas and walked around in socks. There was a man whose joints and limbs were frozen in catatonic space—even his eyes wouldn't move from where they stared at the ceiling. There was another man who kept trying to flirt with me, trying to impress me with the fact that he'd almost become a fire-fighter. (I didn't believe him.) There were one too many depressed and suicidal drug addicts suffering from their own withdrawals.Sometimes we were allowed to ask permission to call someone. There were only three phones, so at those times, it was difficult to actually *get* the phone. I waited until the firefighter was done talking to his mom, overhearing bits of his conversation. When would I talk to Rob again?

I knew what I needed to say, had been practicing it in my head whenever I thought about the two of us wrestling, his restraining me, in the hotel bathroom. I didn't want him to break the engagement—oh, please, please no—but he needed to.

"You can leave me, Rob. You have an out," I said as soon as he picked up.

I didn't want to start crying, but I did. I wondered if he had already been thinking about it. Would he say I wasn't the girl he fell in love with? Was I? As much as I didn't want to be like the others in the crazy ward, here I was, in my pajamas holding onto a cold, yellow telephone in the hall of a mental hospital.

"What are you talking about?" He knew what I was talking about.

"I'm saying you have an out. I won't be mad at you. I understand—everyone will understand. You don't have to do this."

"Don't ever say that again."

"But—"

"I'm never leaving. I love you. Do you hear me? Don't ever say that again."

"But how do you know what you want? Maybe we're too young... You have to be smart, right? You have to do what's right for *you*. I get it. I do." I started sobbing.

"I'm not going anywhere."

"You shouldn't have to keep *your fiancée* from banging into walls, Rob. I'm *so* sorry."

"I'm not going anywhere. I'm gonna love you even when it isn't easy. You already know that."

"You're being stupid."

"I'm not going anywhere."

~

Being *out* of the hospital was harder than being *in*.

I stood underneath the spray of water in my dorm's shower, feeling the pressure of it on my shoulders and against my back. How long had I been in the shower? Ten minutes? Two hours? Two minutes? I studied my toes for a while longer and then turned the water off.

I sat on the floor in my towel and counted the number of long ash brown hairs, escaped from my hairbrush, in the crevices of the tile. I needed to clean the bathroom, but I couldn't, not now.

I started to cry. I *wanted* to clean the bathroom. Why couldn't I clean the bathroom?

I stood up from the floor, ignored the urge. It wasn't logical. It wasn't rational—they all said so. I needed to listen to others right now. Not myself.

I went to my bedroom, still crying and still wrapped in my towel, and folded myself back into bed. It'd been weeks since my discharge, and the mania had crashed right into a depression.

"What now?" I moaned aloud and pulled my duvet over my head. What was going on now? I tried to remember my psychiatrist's words.

"Recovery takes longer than the trauma itself."

How much longer?

I can't do anything. I can't do anything.

I was a seesaw, emotions going up and then going down. Weeping, always weeping. Can't find the canned beans in the grocery store—tears. That person looked at me strangely—tears. Can't make breakfast—tears. No control; no concentration. Forget schoolwork—couldn't focus. At all. A watercolor masterpiece of uselessness and despair. My brain was gray-colored pudding. Wet mortar squished between bricks. Smog.

Soon after I left the hospital, I began cutting my arms and my thighs in the bathroom with shards of glass from a broken cup that I hid in my drawer. I'd broken the cup against the faucet and saved a piece to slide behind the toothpaste and lotions where no would see. I felt bad about hiding it, naughty even.

Rob was back in Colorado and was not witness to my everyday agony. I did my best to keep things light over the phone. But I needed to *see* my pain. I needed to make sense of the loss of control of my own body. I'd heard of people cutting themselves. Never understood it. What does it accomplish? Nothing. But when logic is wiped away and all I'm left with is raw emotion, the need to physically *feel* emotional pain is the *only* thing that makes sense. The scratches on my arms were proof to myself of whatever was cutting up my brain from the inside out.

I wasn't, however, alone.

Mom came.

Mom left her life in Colorado for two months to come and stay with me. In a few weeks, the staff at the small hotel knew her name and her breakfast and coffee order.

She emailed my professors about getting extended due dates, drove me to and from classes, sat in on a few of those classes to take notes for me (I couldn't hold a pen), typed up my papers (I talked, she typed), and hired a tutor to get me through the two-credit math class that could keep me from graduating.

She, at times, took me to meals and, at other times, cooked in our apartment for my roommates and me. She took me to get my nails done every week: "physical thera-py," she called it. She took me to counseling appoint-ments; she monitored my cutting.

Amidst all of this, Mom planned my wedding—bought me a second wedding dress when I second-guessed the first—and found an apartment and furniture for Rob's and my new life together back in Colorado. I couldn't handle thinking about finances, so she paid for everything.

I was twenty-two years old, and my mom was living my life for me.

One evening in December, we were snuggling in her hotel bed watching HGTV. A newly married couple was looking for an "ocean bungalow," and the show's realtor managed a smile despite their negativity. Wife wanted wood floors; husband didn't. The realtor smiled some more.

My mind wandered.

"What are you thinking?" She noticed my glazed look.

"What's the point? The purpose of it all?"

"Well, honey, I don't know."

"How could God do this to me when I clearly couldn't handle it?"

"I know you're hurting."

"My body has betrayed me. Did—did God?"

My mom leaned back into the pillows, and I followed. I was four again, listening to a bedtime story in my mother's arms.

She reminded me of a story in the Old Testament. The Israelites, the main group of people of the text, are engaged in battle with their enemy. Moses, their leader, must keep his arms raised from where he stands, overlooking the fight. If he lowered his arms, the enemy began to win: his strength would determine the outcome. But Moses *does* grow tired. He was too weak to keep his arms raised indefinitely. So, his brother and a friend hold his arms up for him. The Israelites win the battle.

I told her that I couldn't hear God anymore, ever since the hospital. There was silence and there was absence.

"Where is God in pain?"

"You must see Him in the people around you—in me. In Rob. In Dad. That's sometimes how God works. God uses people for His good."

That was enough for me. I could keep my arms up with help; I could hear God in others when I couldn't hear Him elsewhere.

Come to me, you who are weary and burdened. I will give you rest.

~

I survived the semester with my arms raised and returned home two weeks before my wedding. I was fragile, but numb.

I fell into a depression during Christmas and moved about the house slowly, trying to be happy about my graduation and the upcoming unknowns.

I prayed every night that the depression would lift on the day of the wedding. *Please make me feel better. Please let the depression lift, if only for a day.*

God gave it to me—the January wedding was perfect.

Peace I leave you; peace I give to you.

Because I wasn't involved that much in the planning, everything was a surprise: the flowers, the decorations. I'd given my input on colors and that was about it. I think brides turn into she-devils when things don't go as expected, and since I didn't have any expectations, I couldn't have been happier. The lack of booze (a tribute to my grandmother's presence) displeased many, but *I* was in a daze, and *everything* was perfect. Rob and I left the wedding early, feigning fatigue, interested only in each other. I told myself that things were finally going as planned, that God was good. I had my man, and that longing for love would finally be fulfilled. I told myself that the New Year could only be better than the one before. During my wedding, I wasn't bipolar. I was the bride.

11

———

I dreaded the start of every day. I dreaded the end of every day, because that meant I'd have to begin all over again.

It was time to get my nails done. On Tuesday. That was Tuesday. If I could manage to get myself out of bed, then maybe I could go to the gym's pool. Swim a bit, come home, sit on the couch and wait. I wouldn't blow dry my hair, because the dryer was too heavy to hold and because the five minutes felt like two hours. So, instead, I'd go over to my mom's for an afternoon with wet hair and wait again, at her stainless-steel kitchen table, until she had time to paint my nails a soft mauve color. Each nail took a few minutes—which felt like three, four, five hours—and I stared at the TV, trying to push down the confused emotion pushing at my throat.

Tick. Tock.

I'd return home and wait yet again, this time for Rob to return home from work. Look at the clock. Try to read a book and fail. Look at the clock again. I lived nine Tuesdays in less than twenty-four hours, and all nine felt long and empty.

The clock on the stove, the time on my phone, the clock on my car's radio—they all taunted me. I feared empty spaces of time, felt anxious whenever I had nothing to *do,* which was *all the time.* Even at night, I feared being unable to fall asleep because of the daunting hours of *just lying* there. My psychiatrist had me popping anxiety medication regularly, which, though it helped me sleep, did little to help the underlying paralyzing depression that had ensnared me after our wedding.

They all wanted me to rest. You've been through trauma, my parents said. You need to take care of yourself, Rob said. You're not able to hold a job right now, the psychiatrist said. I was told to take a year off.

A year off of *what*? Life?

They all came up with ideas for me to do—learning to cook, a freelance writing project for my grandfather, an aerobics dance class—but all of those things seemed to take too much of the energy I didn't have. I cried if I burnt something on the stove. I stared dumbly at my grandfather's notes and the blank Word document. I couldn't jump up and down to music—I could barely lie on my back.

~

I decided to clean the apartment. I worked up the nerve to approach the Lysol spray beneath the sink. When I realized it was gone—Rob must have used the last of it—I knew I wouldn't be able to get myself to the store or make a water and vinegar mixture that would do the job instead. It took me half an hour to clean the granite island countertop.

One hour later, (which felt like five hours), I unplugged the vacuum and wrapped the chord before placing it on the hook. There. Something done. The vacuum grinned at me; it was a wicked grin, and I began to sob and sank to the laundry room floor.

Was this my life now? I was a college graduate. I was a married woman. And my entire day could be summarized by two hours of cleaning the apartment I couldn't get myself to leave. *You're pathetic.*

I feared meeting someone I knew—an old acquaintance, one of Rob's coworkers.

"What do you do?" The dreaded question.

"Unemployed for now."

"Just taking some time off."

"Writing." A lie.

~

R ob and I sat at the kitchen table at the same time every evening.

I swallowed a few more spoonfuls of my second bowl of soup. I thought I was putting on weight rapidly (I wasn't) and felt powerless to stop it. Each bite equaled another moment of hating myself later that night.

"How was your day?" he asked. He had just finished telling me about his own day, the classes that went poorly and then ones that went well. They were halfway through

Lord of the Flies, and only half of the students had turned in their essays on time.

"My day? The same as usual." I swam that morning (floated) and read a few pages of a novel. Oh, and made the soup. *So* productive.

"What can I do to make you feel better?" He always asked me this, and I gave him the same answer every time.

"You can't."

"I want to help you. Let me help you."

"You can't." I knew he couldn't. No matter what he said, it couldn't fix the numbness hanging about my head.

Rob looked away. Stared at the *Friends* episode playing on the TV by the couch. It was a circle, the way we went around and around my problems.

He looked back at me. "You know I love you." He'd said the same thing the night before, when he caught me poking at my bare flabby stomach in the bathroom mirror, disgust all over my face.

"I know. I love you too."

I did love him. A lot. There was nothing wrong with the marriage. Our bond, formed by the trauma months earlier, could not be stronger.

Marriage did not solve my problems. It did not help my depression. It did not make me feel better about my body like our romance once had in the early months of the relationship.

To clarify: I didn't get married to solve my mental health, but I certainly had thought it would.

Wasn't marriage, after all, the goal? For the entirety of my life, I had wanted to be loved.

Rob's love, and this sacred institution we'd entered together, was supposed to be the culmination of all my desires.

It wasn't.

My life did not magically become better. It became worse, not because of the marriage, but in spite of our newfound happiness together. The happiness I felt with Rob could not defeat the depression and self-hatred that took over.

Rob's and my love for one another did not satiate my hunger for *something better*. I found myself *still* craving love, longing for love. Love for what? Of what? Maybe when the depression left, I would feel silly for wanting something nonexistent.

I turned whatever energy I had in me to pleasing Rob as best I could. Making his breakfast in the morning, folding his clean laundry twice a week: little gifts I could manage. It was the best I could do. I couldn't be the happy, normal me, so I needed to make up for it somehow. I focused on making him happy since I couldn't be happy myself.

Later that spring, we planned a trip to England for a few weeks—since Rob was a teacher, he had the summer off—and prayed for a lifted and stable mood. We wanted to avoid another episode and hoped a vacation would do me good.

"What can I do to make you feel better?" England would be the answer.

~

And God?

I couldn't understand why He'd let everything happen the way it did, but I knew He was still around. Somehow. I couldn't hear Him anymore and I didn't know why, but I kept praying and praying anyway. That's what faith was. Doubt felt unimportant when compared to my needed prayers for healing.

"I won't give up my faith," I told my mom one nail-painting afternoon. A dark gray color this time, a trend I was trying. "I won't do that." I thought of Moses with his arms raised.

Resolve came out of somewhere, from my upbringing, perhaps, or maybe somewhere real.

"He loves you, Anna. He's in this," she said.

I studied the dark clump of paint at the corner of my thumb. Didn't she see it?

"Yeah, I guess. I mean, you don't have to tell me that."

God's love. Blah, blah, blah. I knew all that. Right now, I needed to focus on faith. Trust, not love.

In the midst of the depression, I needed to trust God. That's what I believed. He'd see my faith and be proud of me. He'd know I deserve His healing. But why did it feel like He was disappearing?

~

The jeans squeezed into my stomach, forcing my nasty flesh over the top of my pants like an over-stuffed bag of thick peach jelly. I couldn't force my eyes away from reflective windows as we walked through London, couldn't "un-feel" my middle. Each window: fat, fat, fat.

I couldn't even look at the size on the tag in my jeans —it was too triggering. Numbers equaled identity. High equaled evil.

Before our train ride to Edinburgh, I told Rob I wanted to buy some new clothes to match the British fashion. I couldn't bear to tell him that I was unable to button my jeans. He made fun of me, laughing about my overflowing suitcase, but said he didn't care what I wanted to buy.

Even with the new clothes, I pinched myself, hard, again and again in the shower. How dare you eat that second scone. How dare you feel pretty when you're not. How dare *you*. I didn't stop eating—not once. I just punished myself when I did eat.

Rob so badly wanted to enjoy our vacation.

"You're having fun, right?" he asked.

"You seem like you're feeling better."

"We're having a great time, aren't we, Anna?"

I carried the depression around, dragging it behind me like my suitcase on London's busy streets, but this time without wheels. Forced smiles. Feigned interest.

I tried making myself feel better by online job searching on my phone in-between museums. If I found something to do, I would feel better. I was organized. Efficient. An executive assistant—that could be me.

Rob tried to persuade me to wait. Told me I wasn't ready yet. The stress could break me.

He was wrong. If I were busy, time wouldn't pass so

slowly. Maybe busyness could conquer sadness. I *had* to have a job, and quickly. I needed to distract myself.

As soon as we returned home, I began the search with urgency, applying and emailing and applying some more. Rob found me hunched over my computer at the white desk in our room each afternoon, and he knew I'd been there for hours, obsessed. He told me I was getting worked up about something that could wait, that I wasn't ready yet. I didn't listen.

Applying to jobs gave me a sort of weird energy. The rush gave me a few days relief from my depression. I had several successful interviews for a church receptionist job, met the pastors wearing my new black pencil skirt and red blazer, but just as I felt ready to accept the job, the *feeling* set in. I rescinded my application, knowing I was incapable of a full-time position if I were truly depressed.

As a last-ditch effort, I tried getting a job in retail—something I thought I couldn't possibly screw up—but when my second shift came around, I couldn't even get out of bed. I had to call the manager and apologize over and over about quitting so abruptly.

"I'm sick," I tried weakly.

"Sick? Sick? Then why don't you take some medicine and come into work?"

She fumed at me, muttering about a millennial's sense of entitlement, until I hung up on her, completely humiliated.

It felt like it came out of nowhere, simply because I'd had a brief respite from the depression. But it'd been building for some time, waiting for the perfect moment to run its dull scissors across my throat. Why did it happen again? There's no logic to it. There's no logic to bipolar.

It was darker and deeper than I'd ever had before. It was more than self-hatred, more than sadness. It felt physical, tactile. It was too much, all at once, one giant block of endless agony.

Depression, this *feeling*, was like getting stuck in traffic in 100-degree weather with no air-conditioning. Standing in mud, sinking a half an inch at a time. My kidneys exploding, again and again and again. Crouched in a cardboard box, listening to someone tape it shut. My ribs shrinking and expanding at sporadic times. Carrying skis uphill but not making any progress. Someone holding my head under water. Being slowly adrift in space, watching the earth spin below, knowing I wouldn't touch it again. Standing with my arms outstretched to the sides, unable to lower them. Hearing a loud, screaming silence and absolutely nothing else. Standing in line, watching others cut in front of me. Looking at someone with the most intense hatred I've ever felt (at myself). A black plastic table crushing my chest into the floor. All at the same time.

I couldn't leave the house. I couldn't leave the couch. I couldn't roll over. All I wanted was to not feel anymore, to die.

～

No other voice this time. It's just me. Alone. Here. Present tense again.

I feel every cell of my body. Each one groans, moans complaints at me. I feel the underneath of my skin. It's too tight—it feels like charred leather. My mind hurts. Oh, it hurts.

I want to die. I want this to be over. I can't take it anymore.

I try to turn my head towards Rob where he sits on the couch, and I tell him that I want my life to end. I don't want to feel the pain, and there is no other way. No other way, Rob. No fucking other way.

I crave nothing. Nothing, where this doesn't exist. Darkness. Peace.

He tells me to stop talking like that, crying and begging me to talk to my doctor. Or my parents. Anybody.

I decide. Right there. I decide and I have a plan now and it will all be over soon and I can finally not *feel* this anymore and I've decided.

Rob gets up, goes to the bathroom.

Now.

Strength from nowhere fills my limbs, and I leave the living room, out the door, to the garage, in the car. Adrenaline, but from where? Doesn't matter. The car is on, and this time the garage is small.

Now I have no concept of time. Anyway, what is time in terms of nothingness? Just a matter of time until, what, no time?

My phone buzzes from my pocket.

anna where are u

    anna come back

    im trying to find u

    please stop whatever ur doing

    come back

    hold on im coming

    where are u

    im looking for u

    come back

He calls me. Why do I answer?

"It's over, Rob. This is it. I'm sorry. I'm saying goodbye."

He starts screaming at me.

"It's okay, this is what I want. I don't want to feel anymore." I'm crying, but I'm calm.

He's begging now. Pleading. Bargaining.

"I'm so sorry."

"Anna—I can NOT live without you. Do you understand that? Don't do this to me."

This time, I hear him. I realize that my action will hurt him more than it will hurt me. *Don't do this to me.* This would destroy Rob.

I turn off the engine, stumble from the garage, and fall on the ground. I feel nothing, just like I wanted, but I know I failed.

There, on the ground, I am so alone. I peeked at

death, and I didn't blink, in a shallow space between heaven and hell—in a space where neither one existed. I looked—a simple ten-second glance, not a stare—at death, and it was nothingness. I was completely and utterly alone. God wasn't there.

~

Rob convinced me to go to the hospital the next day. I was compliant at first, but once I was checked in, I panicked. I begged the doctors to let me leave, but they refused. I didn't complete the suicide attempt, they said, but I'd started. That was enough to keep me.

I'd never pleaded for anything before, not like that. I actually got onto my knees, in the praying position, begging them to let me go.

"I won't try again, I promise. Please let me leave. I don't want to be here. I promise I'll be safe."

They didn't believe me.

I called my parents, but they, too, would not vouch for me.

"I hate you," I screamed at my mom. "You're betraying me."

I went to the room I now shared with another patient and cried until I fell into an exhausted sleep. I woke, refused dinner and a therapist session, and lay face down, crying again into my thin, perforated pillow.

I thought about earlier, when I'd tried to die. Where was God then? Where was His voice? He had betrayed me too.

"God is dead. God is dead. God is dead." I pounded my fist into the blanket.

It was over, God and me. There was no *something better*. God was dead.

~

The month after the hospital was worse than the one before. Surprise, surprise. Medications did not work as quickly as predicted, and my depression deepened. But this time, I didn't even have the energy to kill myself. There was no will to live, but there was nothing I could do about it. I clung to Rob each evening, begging him to help me, when we both knew he couldn't.

My therapist helped me plan one thing to do a day. The day was a success if I went on a walk, took one nap instead of two, or talked to someone on the phone. I experienced panic attacks any time I drove my car, but therapy helped me with that as well. It was embarrassing, how reliant I became on my counselor. I paid her $150.00 an hour just so that I could drive to and from her office without crying. But what else could I do?

My therapist encouraged me to spend time with my sister, so I did. Abby and I sat with cups of tea at her kitchen table or with paint and easels in her upstairs loft. She was dealing with her chronic migraines, unable to hold a job, just like me. The migraines had taken over my loud, outgoing sister just like bipolar had taken over me.

Abby had been to specialty clinics; she was on so many drugs that she lost count. Still, her migraines continued to worsen. One doctor told her that she should only do an hour of work a day, lest she damage herself further. Grocery shopping? There went her hour. Lunch with me? There went her hour. Still, she pushed herself in her writing, determined to find joy in *something*.

I felt like I understood her better; because of my depression, I *saw* her for maybe the first time. My beautiful, intelligent sister, confined to her house. She was wading through her hurt, trying to cling to her beliefs.

"You know that song, the Kelly Clarkson one that goes *whatever doesn't kill you makes you stronger*?" she asked me one afternoon.

"Yeah."

"It's bullshit. My migraines haven't killed me—yet—but they haven't made me stronger. Not one bit. They just make me weaker and weaker, the worse they get."

"Do you think there is a purpose in all of this?"

"I don't think there can ever be a simple answer to that question."

Abby and I never officially made up after our fight two years prior, but our illnesses gave us something in common. We knew what hurt felt like, so we knew each other. Empathy planted; friendship bloomed. She's the only one who understood how I could sit in a chair and not move for hours, staring at the wall or crying because I couldn't get myself to stand up. She understood that I could laugh, but not really laugh, at the same time. She understood what it felt like to be a burden on her husband. Abby, the friend-enemy of my childhood, became a best friend.

When I was in the hospital, I'd overheard a conversation between two other patients. One guy was talking about his bipolar ex-wife and how he just "couldn't take it anymore" and "had to do what was right for himself." He had to leave his wife for his own well-being. So, at home, I watched Rob carefully, wary of any pitying looks or frustrating sighs. I think I knew, deep down somewhere, he wouldn't leave me, just as my mom hadn't left my dad years ago, but the fear was there anyway. I couldn't help but worry about him. Rob had been through the trauma with me, yet he didn't go to a counselor or confide in anyone else. He carried the weight on his shoulders, ever the hero, and I wondered if, one day, he would break.

⁓

As usual with bipolar, the depression eventually lifted. That's the nature of the cycle. One just has to be patient, and things *do* get better. The waiting period is the hardest, but if you can make yourself get through it —or if others can get you through it—life tastes joy once again.

I went to therapy and took my medicine like I was supposed to. Talked to Rob, cried with Rob. Applied to grad school. Got a puppy that made my life harder before it got better. Didn't stop hating my body but got a control on the self-harm. (For a while.) Days slid into one another, and time became unimportant.

Three breakdowns. *Three.* Bipolar was my reality, and I'd have it the rest of my life. The rest of my life? How could I come to terms with that? I liked to say, "I have bipolar," instead of "I am bipolar." The simple nuance gave me a sense of distance from the disease.

Yet in all of this, even with the depression gone, I was exceedingly unhappy. I'd lost my faith, my purpose, and I didn't know what to replace it with. My faith—an actual relationship—was gone. It was like a friend—my confidant—had died. Broken up with me. I missed the easy faith of my adolescence, the way I'd managed to trust despite my doubts.

Rob and I managed to continue our love-filled and content life together, even after everything that had happened—and it still wasn't enough. My soul was dark, silent. My God was gone.

12

"You gave yourself a concussion on purpose?" The doctor looked up from her clipboard. Her white coat was immaculate, but her black slacks were covered in tiny gray hairs. A cat, probably. Two cats.

"So, it's a concussion?" I didn't want to tell her the truth about how the headaches had started because she'd probably refer to me a psychiatrist. She'd probably give me *that look*. But it felt wrong, somehow, to lie to a doctor when she asked how it happened.

"And yeah... on purpose." I paused again. "You know, like head banging."

The doctor held her pen in mid-air.

"But you don't have to be concerned," I said. "I'm already working with my psychiatrist, and I just started with a new therapist. So, it's fine. It won't happen again."

I could tell she didn't know what to say as she pursed her lips, wrote something else on the clipboard, and stood to leave.

"You only have one brain, you know," she said.

"I know."

"You need to take care of it. Your brain, that is. You clearly have a concussion."

"I figured."

"You need to rest. No work, no exercise. Just resting your head. I'll prescribe some pain medicine." She gave me the disapproving eyes—*the look*—and turned to leave. "Okay then, take care."

I was afraid she'd return with a security guard and handcuffs. I knew I probably sounded crazy. What kind of person rams her head into the bathroom counter? Over and over and over? That was a month ago, and the headaches still persisted. Pounding in my temples and behind my eyes.

I left the doctor's office, avoiding the nurse's gaze just in case he'd overheard, and went to my car. I sat, leaned against the window, and closed my eyes. The pounding didn't stop.

A month ago, Rob and I took a long weekend in the mountains. It was supposed to be a quiet weekend for the both of us: out of the house and into some fresh mountain air. The orange fall colors were gone, and ski season had yet to begin, so there weren't many visitors. Most things in the little tourist town were closed. But there was a tennis court, a hot tub, hiking trails: everything needed for a relaxing mini-vacation.

It wasn't relaxing at all.

I was depressed again. It was a year after the suicide attempt, and I was depressed once more. Not that I'd been depressed the entire year—it'd gone away for a while—but I was getting used to a mood episode every fall. That was the pattern of the last three years.

What was it about the seasons?

Sometimes I imagined that my bipolar disorder has a long cord connected to the sun. It's a thick cord, steel, and tinted yellow from the light. As the earth tilts away from the sun, something moves inside my brain.

I tried to enjoy our stay in the mountains, but maybe the lack of sunlight had too much pull on my chemistry. My brain tried to make sense of the feeling and created a culprit.

I *hated* my body. Hated it. I was obsessed with hating it. I had put on weight during the first two years of marriage, and I could tell by the way my clothes were fitting. The depression accentuated this hatred, made it more intense, more unbearable.

So, when Rob was getting something from the car, and when I was alone in the room, I punished myself. I scratched my legs with the edge of a lotion bottle (those scratches would disappear, and Rob would never know), and I hit my head into the granite countertop. *This will teach you.* It was a punishment; it was my escape. Maybe if I hit my head hard enough, the feelings would go away, and I could be skinny again.

∾

Hitting my head made no sense—it accomplished nothing. I knew that. But it's what I did, and I had a month of lying on the couch with an icepack to think about it before the headaches subsided.

Though it was certainly affected by my moods, I can't say that my body hatred was purely a part of the mood issue. That just wouldn't be true. I'd later try to explore the root of my hatred, not as a part of bipolar disorder but as an eating disorder of its own. Where had it come from? Had it been around since I was fourteen? When the eating disorder flares, is it a precursor to a mood episode?

I was frustrated with myself and, frankly, with my own honesty. I couldn't blame this all on bipolar. I wanted to, because it would be easy, but I couldn't. My body was my personal demon. At times I tried to fight the hatred—I *did*—but it often felt too helpless. The eating disorder was an addiction: it's something I desperately wanted to stop, but couldn't.

Once, I was standing before the mirror naked, crying. What I saw was not acceptable. "Not acceptable": that's what I kept telling myself.

Rob came in and put his arm on my shoulder. We stood there together, quiet, before he spoke.

"What will happen if we have a daughter, and she comes to you because the girls say she isn't pretty?"

"I never want her to feel the way I do."

"Why can't you treat yourself like you'd treat her?"

I would *never* tell my daughter that she is "not acceptable." I would *never* bang her head against the wall. I would *never* scratch her arms and legs as a punishment for her looks, like I did to my own arms. I wouldn't look at her stomach with disgust. I would look at her with nothing but love.

~

As time went on, and the suicide attempt faded into the past, I improved and slowly gained myself back.

There were fluxes with the seasons, but they weren't been full-blown. In the spring before the concussion, I had felt the high of a hypomania. I dyed my hair blonde on a whim, spent hours shopping online, and went to a tanning bed as a middle finger to my health, but the small episode was harmless. I knew enough to say something to my psychiatrist, and, with a medication adjustment, I felt normal in a few weeks. The hypomania was never really anything, never really got dangerous.

The depression that came afterwards was hard and the concussion was annoying, but the headaches, too, didn't last long.

Maybe I started to get a handle on the whole bipolar thing. I'd like to think that one day, I won't even need to adjust medication. I'll have the perfect cocktail, and it'll be nothing more than taking my morning vitamins.

...No. It will never be easy. Bipolar is a chronic illness. I now deal with it responsibly with medication and therapy—that's the right thing to do, they say, and I like being the good girl. But it will always dominate at least a corner of my life. I can't have high stress. I have to make sure I stay on a sleep schedule. I have to avoid movies and shows with too much emotion or gore. I have to protect myself.

~

Surprisingly, it was being in a church small group that made me feel the most pathetic. "Small group" is Christian lingo for fellowship outside of the church service. In my opinion, it was more like a forced gathering with people who normally wouldn't be friends outside of church. Most churches facilitate small groups nowadays, making this nothing special, but Rob and I were new to the group.

Everyone was sitting around a guy's living room, coffee and donuts balanced in hands and in laps, and chairs squeezed closely together to make room for the large, fake, white Christmas tree.

Rob and I listened to their conversation, not really knowing how to jump in. They were talking about a white elephant gift exchange at the pastor's house, about all the silly and weird gifts that had been unwrapped. A large pink plunger. A stuffed armadillo. Since Rob and I hadn't been at the party, we didn't have much to contribute.

"And then there was this one gift—tell them about that one," one woman nudged another in the arm. "Tell them about that weird book."

"Oh yeah. That one." The other woman laughed. "I opened one gift and it was this, this... book. This book about," she made a face, "about *bipolar people*."

Everyone in the room laughed.

I can't really explain the feeling that settled itself into my chest, but there it was, heavy and large.

I was a freak. I was a joke. I was something funny.

~

Later that afternoon, on a walk around the lake near our house, Rob fumed about the whole exchange, tugging on our dog's leash just a little too harshly.

He couldn't believe the insensitivity. Couldn't believe they'd laughed at something that shouldn't have been funny.

"Don't half of people with bipolar try to commit suicide? How is something fatal *funny?* They don't joke about cancer—why do they joke about this?"

People tend to laugh at things they don't understand. Bipolar can sound scary—weird—and people laugh when they encounter something so *different*, something foreign. (Is instability something they should find hilarious or frightening? What does bipolar even mean?) I knew that they had no idea about my situation. We didn't need to overreact—I was aware of this too.

But their laughter made me feel self-conscious, as if I really *was* worthy of laughter.

I tell myself that our culture's attitude towards mental illness is changing—now, depression and anxiety are not as shameful as they once were—but I get discouraged about how slow that progress is.

We stopped going to the small group. When my parents asked me about it, I told them it was because we just didn't fit in, didn't click with them. It was sort of true. I didn't want to admit that the group's laughter had hurt too deeply for me to return.

~

I kept going to church with Rob, even though I told him that I didn't believe anymore.

I stood during worship, but I did not sing. I bowed my head, but I did not pray. I shook hands, but I never made eye contact. Communion tasted bitter in my mouth.

Faith was important to Rob, so I didn't want to stop our churchgoing abruptly. It wouldn't be only my life that disbelief would interrupt: it would be *our* life. He understood how I felt, never pressured me to change my mind, but he was glad for the pretense.

Months went by; I felt my heart harden. I became fixated with the idea of *nothingness*. Nothing: it scared me and thrilled me at the same time. I didn't know what it meant. When I thought about God, I just got angry.

~

And then something strange happened. It's difficult to explain, because it happened so quickly and because, well, honestly, because now it seems rather silly. But to forget it, to act like nothing happened, is simply cheating myself.

I'd woken one night to go the bathroom. Nothing new, but I was mad that I was so wide-awake. It would take me an hour to fall asleep again.

On my way back to bed, something pushed against me, made me take a step back. It startled me, and I froze. My eyes strained in the darkness, now fully awake. Nothing was there. So why did I feel like I was staring at something?

The room was hot and stuffy, but goose bumps prickled my bare skin; cold sweat broke into instant beads on my forehead. I wasn't alone.

Anna.

I stretched my arms out in front of me, waved my fingers in the air. Something was in front of me. Or was it now behind me? It was a kind of presence, and it was all around me. It was quiet. It was tangible, and it wasn't at the same time.

I'm here.

Anna, I will never forsake you.

I stood there for a few minutes, unmoving, trying to hear something spoken yet unspoken. Finally, the space around me seemed to relax, to sag back into normalcy, and I went—ran—into bed. I woke Rob up and in urgent whispers told him what happened.

There, I told him, in the darkness, something—something familiar—was there. I couldn't deny it. The feeling was too real, too recognizable. It was like I'd just met something (someone?) that I'd forgotten I'd known.

"I have to believe, Rob. I have to." I didn't think through what I was saying. It happened so quickly—was there even anything to process? Rob mumbled a response and rolled over. I stared at the ceiling, feeling so many things at once: uncertainty, assurance, fear, excitement.

I don't understand it and I never will, but there *was* some kind of encounter. Again, maybe it seems silly. I was tired; maybe it was nothing. But maybe it wasn't. Maybe it's arrogant to say that, just because I don't understand something, it doesn't exist.

When I woke up the next morning, I was more angry

than confused. He was calling me back, by name, just as He'd called me when I was a child. I didn't want to be called.

~

My unbelief was never unbelief. It was anger.

God was never just an idea to me—He was a something, a someone, I'd known my entire life. I'd bargained with Him, pleaded with Him, loved Him. So, when bipolar happened, and happened again, and *again*, I wanted to reject God, this "someone" that I felt had betrayed me. It was easier to not believe in God than to know that I hated Him.

I hated God because He promised me in a dream that I'd have *something better*. Who promises a kid, or lets her think she has a promise, for something good, when she'll never get to see it? Why let me go on thinking that?

For I know the plans I have for you, to give you hope and a future.

I hated God because He let me lose my mind. Not once, not twice, but three times. Three times, God, three times. *Why have you forsaken me?*

I will never leave you, nor will I forsake you.

I hated God because bipolar would always be a part of my life. Chronic pain, for the rest of my life, just like my sister.

What is seen is temporary. What is unseen is eternal.

I hated God because of my disappointment with men. No man's love was enough. No man could truly fulfill me.

I am the way. I am the truth. I am the life.

I hated God because I *still* was not as beautiful as I wanted.

I knit you together in your mother's womb: my works are wonderful.

I hated God because, even though I tried to follow Him my whole life, from the time I was a child, He didn't keep me from harm. What was my faithfulness worth? Nothing?

I will turn your mourning into dancing.

~

In the Christian tradition, there are different seasons of faith. There is one advanced season that some people never even come to, one that is probably the most difficult. It is called "The Dark Night of the Soul."

In this stage, God purposely stands back: He becomes absent. He purposely hides Himself and removes His consolations (or felt comfort) from the individual. A person is left with a feeling of abandonment, because the voice of God is silent, gone.

Mother Teresa, the saint who devoted her entire life to God, is said to have experienced this stage *for years*. There she was, serving her Lord, all the while feeling like He'd abandoned her. In the Old Testament, in Psalm 88, the Sons of Korah wrote a whole song dedicated to the dark night of the soul.

Jesus experienced His dark night of the soul as He bore the weight of humanity on the cross. He was alone, in the pain, in the darkness, when He cried out to God. *Why have You forsaken Me?*

But there is purpose in this season. Though the world is fallen, and though sometimes illness and pain just happen, God is still working in the silence and in our anger. He is there, in the nighttime, when we cry and when we shake our fists. One purpose is for us to realize just how desperately we need and desire a relationship with Him. He longs for us, just as we long for Him.

And when does God relent?

There is always another side, eventually, here on earth or in the afterlife. I cling to that truth. Some have to wait longer than others.

> I wait for the Lord, my whole being waits,
> and in his word I put my hope.
> I wait for the Lord
> more than watchmen wait for the
> morning,
> more than watchmen wait for the
> morning.
> Psalm 130:5-6

I knew about this stage, and I began to think that I might be in the midst of it. So I took time away, to think. To doubt. I went to church, sat, and listened to silence. Came home, sat, and listened to the silence. Life goes on, as it's prone to do, and time gave me the space I needed. The hatred began to dissipate; I accepted my anger. My dark night of the soul became a sacred place, and I began to hear God once more.

~

I crave love. I always have, as a child, a teenager, a young woman. I think I cared too much about it. All those silly boys... how embarrassing that I made such a fuss! The infatuation—it seems so silly now. I guess bipolar forced me to finally grow up. Love—and my faith —I see it all so differently now.

It's human nature to want to feel loved, so I'll give myself a break. The love I wanted is something I still want. But now, I don't want it from a man.

I don't think my craving will ever be satisfied while I walk on earth. Even Rob, my beloved, devoted, trust-worthy Rob, is not enough. There is a longing; it's a divine sort of longing that still haunts me: it is a longing for God.

But how do I embrace God's love when I can't even love myself?

One day. *One day.*

There's a word in German: *Fernweh*. It's a word that many theologians say they wish we had in English. *Fernweh* is an aching for somewhere you've never been before, a longing for something you don't even know.

That's it. That's what my craving feels like. It's an ache for something *other*.

I long for the love of God that I already have, the love of God I don't, and probably will never, understand. It's my *something better*. It's what gives me just enough purpose to keep caring.

How blessed are all those who long for Me.

~

I f I take any old regular Bible and open the text right to the middle, I will most likely open right to the Psalms. The Psalms are a collection of poetry—once songs, I guess—and many are written by the famous King David.

When most people think of the Psalms, they think of songs of praise. *Hallelujah! Praise the Lord, oh my Soul!*

But there are other psalms that, at least in church, are usually neglected. They're called the Psalms of Lament. They hold bitterness and sadness, frustration and desperation.

I'd never really noticed them before reading about them in Kathleen Norris' *The Cloister Walk*. The book reminded me of their presence.

> O Lord, God of my Salvation
> I have cried out day and night before You.
> Let my prayer come before You;
> Incline Your ear to my cry.
> For my soul is full of troubles,
> And my life draws near to the grave...
> ...You have laid me in the lowest pit,
> In Darkness, in the depths.
> Your wrath lies heavy upon me...
> Psalm 88:1-3,6-7

The Psalmist cries out to God, in a dark night of the soul, for a show of integrity; the Psalmist often complains of being ignored. To be honest, I used to find these Psalms a little unsettling. They seemed audacious, too angry to be addressing the God of the universe. Isn't it wrong to feel angry with God?

But now, I think I understand them.

When the Psalmist shakes his fist, he's simply begging for attention. When he yearns for punishment for his enemies, he's asking for fairness, justice. When he cries out, he doesn't need an answer—he just wants to be heard.

He just wants to be heard.

In the Psalms, God's responses are not recorded. There is lament after lament and no answer. Until, of course, the laments turn into praise as they always do.

ACKNOWLEDGMENTS

As with any writing project, the number of people who have helped and encouraged me are too many to name in the short space below. Please know that I am thankful to each one of you who has helped me to write my story.

When my advisor asked me what I was going to write a book about, I told him, "I don't know, but I do know that the book *won't* be about God." I am thankful for my graduate school experience—I found spiritual reconciliation at such an unlikely place. It was there that this book was conceived, labored over, born, and born again. Thank you to my parents for giving me the opportunity to learn to write.

I am grateful for the girlfriends who have walked with me, as only girlfriends can. For Leigha, Elizabeth, Brooke, Emma, Alyssa, Katy, and Jodi. Each one of you celebrates my writing in your own way and it does not go unnoticed. I love you all so dearly.

I am grateful for the game night crew. For Eli and Naomi, Sam and Ashley, Kellie and now Kyle. You cheered me on as I wrote and re-wrote, and you cele-brated with me when I finished. You are and will always be my people.

And, of course, I am thankful for family. To the Stadick clan (Bill, Judy, Debbie, Kniff, Katie, David, Scott, and Nicole) I want to say: thank you for the unflinching acceptance and for putting up with personal questions. For the Shane gang (Mom, Dad, Abby, Randy, Emma, Ian, and Elly) there is so much that can be said here, but I will leave it at this: you created the loving space for me to grow into myself, and for that I am grateful.

I want to single out my sister Abby, as this book is dedicated to her. Abby, you sat with me in coffee shops and in living rooms and in kitchens—brainstorming, editing, troubleshooting, and formatting this book. You helped me see the tiny details and you helped me see the bigger picture. You have been my cheerleader from the beginning and you've cheered it right through the finish line. You are a gifted writer, a true craftsman, and you inspire me. Thank you.

Now, for Rob. My dearest and my darling. My love. You have given me unwavering support on this project, believing in me when I didn't believe in myself. (A lot of the time.) You are the voice of wisdom in my life, the encourager, the steady one I consistently rely on. Thank you for reminding me of W.S. Merwin's advice, "if you have to be sure [whether it's any good] don't write." Thank you for loving me well.

Lastly, for my children, Auden and George. May you always read and tell good stories. May you always see God in your own story.

ABOUT THE AUTHOR

Anna Shane Stadick lives in Denver, Colorado with her husband, Rob; her two sons, Auden and George; and her dog, Beowulf. Anna spends her time cooking, going on walks in the neighborhood, taking bubble baths, and beating her friends at cards. Check out her blog at annashanestadick.com.

9 780578 912493